THE SHRINKING MIDDLE CLASS

WHY AMERICA IS BECOMING A TWO-CLASS SOCIETY

EMANUEL COLLADO

IUNIVERSE, INC.
NEW YORK   BLOOMINGTON

The Shrinking Middle Class
Why America is becoming a Two-Class Society

The information, ideas, and suggestions in this book are not intended to render professional advice. Before following any suggestions contained in this book, you should consult your personal accountant or other financial advisor. Neither the author nor the publisher shall be liable or responsible for any loss or damage allegedly arising as a consequence of your use or application of any information or suggestions in this book.

iUniverse books may be ordered through booksellers or by contacting:

iUniverse
1663 Liberty Drive
Bloomington, IN 47403
www.iuniverse.com
1-800-Authors (1-800-288-4677)

Because of the dynamic nature of the Internet, any Web addresses or links contained in this book may have changed since publication and may no longer be valid. The views expressed in this work are solely those of the author and do not necessarily reflect the views of the publisher, and the publisher hereby disclaims any responsibility for them.

ISBN: 978-1-4502-1969-3 (sc)
ISBN: 978-1-4502-1968-6 (dj)
ISBN: 978-1-4502-1967-9 (ebk)

Library of Congress Control Number: 2010903731

Printed in the United States of America

iUniverse rev. date: 3/17/2010

ACKNOWLEDGMENTS:

I'd like to express my gratitude to my dad, **Martin Antonio Collado**, and mother, **Ana Julia Collado**, and my older siblings who are **seven brothers** –Elvin, Miguel, Pepe(Peter), Cesar, Fausto, Jose Luis, & Francisco - and **two sisters** – Lidia Mariana and Maria Elena, whose influence and guidance throughout my life have guided me to achieve ultimate goals; to my daughter, **Kaylene Marie Collado**, my pride and joy, to whom I hope to instill a similar vision; To my wife, **Sheree Marie Collado**, who has been there for me during the worst of times. **To all of you reading this book, a BIG HUGE THANK YOU!**

CONTENTS

INTRODUCTION

"The most perfect political community is one in which the middle class is in control, and outnumbers both of the other classes,"
— **Aristotle**

That was Aristotle's take on the middle class somewhere in 350 BC, summing up the importance of that segment of the society. We have come a long, long way after that. But the social fabric remains the same. It is the middle class that acts as the brick and mortar of the society holding the upper class and the lower class together. And what if the middle class crumbles? The society becomes two-tiered with only the upper and the lower classes, only the rich and the poor, without anything binding them. Such a society will eventually crumble. IF our conventional wisdom is right and the middle class really is the social glue that holds society together, then America is in the process of becoming unglued. A middle-class household is frequently defined as one with an income between 75 percent and 125 percent of the median household.

Recently, there has been quite a hue and cry about the US becoming a two-class society, with a shrinking middle class. This trend was first noticed in the 1980s, but was not considered a threat. Almost three decades later, as the US and the world faces economic recession, this particular hitch in the demographics has gained more and more importance with the economists and policy makers. The problem, however, is more financial than social or political. The financial conditions, as existent

1

in the US, is forcing the middle class either to go up the ladder or to come down off it. To understand the causes, repercussions and to take effective measures, one will have to understand the present economic crisis. As the good saying goes: "As you sow, so shall you reap", our past decisions have snowballed in to our present problems.

We shall try and understand what exactly went wrong to have such a disparity in the society – where the social fabric is being skewed to expand at both ends and grow thinner in the middle. And, what does the middle class do in such a situation? The US consists of educated, hard-working people. So learn from previous mistakes, understand the dynamics of money and stop looking up to the government to take care of you. That would be the prescription.

CASE STUDIES OF MIDDLE CLASS FAMILIES

Kim Patterson, 35, runs a successful pre-school institution. Her husband used to work for an MNC as a manager in sales. Their combined earnings were a little over $200,000 per annum. They were a typical happy family with two daughters, both studying in school. The Pattersons had saved a lot in cash and they decided to buy a villa in Orlando. They invested in real estate because, "in real estate prices always go up", or so thought Ms. Patterson. All was fine, till Mr. Patterson lost his job. Within the next six months, the Patterson's' savings was depleted. Unable to run the family and meet the standards of living, they decided to sacrifice their villa and tried to sell it. However, real estate values had dropped and the price of their luxury villa dropped below the mortgage amount. "It is now like a thorn in our throat. We are paying the mortgage and all we can hope is for the prices of real estate to go up," says Ms Patterson. They sold off one of their two cars. They are now facing bankruptcy.

Tony Grant, 38, works as an accountant in a consultancy firm and used to earn a salary of $30,000 per annum. His wife Elisa used to stay at home and look after their three children. "It was okay for us. We used to get by without much of a problem. My salary was enough to go by and I was planning to change my job for a bigger financial institution with a pay hike," says Mr. Grant. A year and a half ago, the firm froze his wages. Six month back, the firm asked all its employees to take a

20 percent cut in pay as expenses were going up to run the firm. Mr. Grant now finds it difficult to sustain his family. "Prices of things have gone up and they have become costly. I could not save much till now and people tell me not to quit my present job as the job market itself seems dull. I don't know what to do," remarks Mr. Grant. Ms Grant now works in a local grocery store to make ends meet and to provide "quality education to (their) children". They family is hoping for the situation to get better so Mr. Grant can leave his current job and try for a better firm with a higher pay.

These two case studies are not sand alone situations. The same problems are being faced by thousands of Americans throughout the US. Cities such as New York and San Francisco are being termed as Super Cities and staying in these places are being considered as a luxury in itself. On the other hand, in places such as Los Angeles and Chicago, cost of living has gone up mostly due to high housing costs. So the middle-income group is squeezed. It is becoming more and more necessary for both the husband and wife to work. However, child care has also become expensive. So the combined income of the family, should now, more than suffice for the costs of bringing up children. For the middle class, quality education is still a necessity. But the cost of education has gone up three to four times in the last couple of decades. So the middle class is finding it difficult to stay in the middle. They either have to go up to a higher level of income, or will have to come down the rungs. So a comparison can be drawn on how the social structure looked yesterday from today.

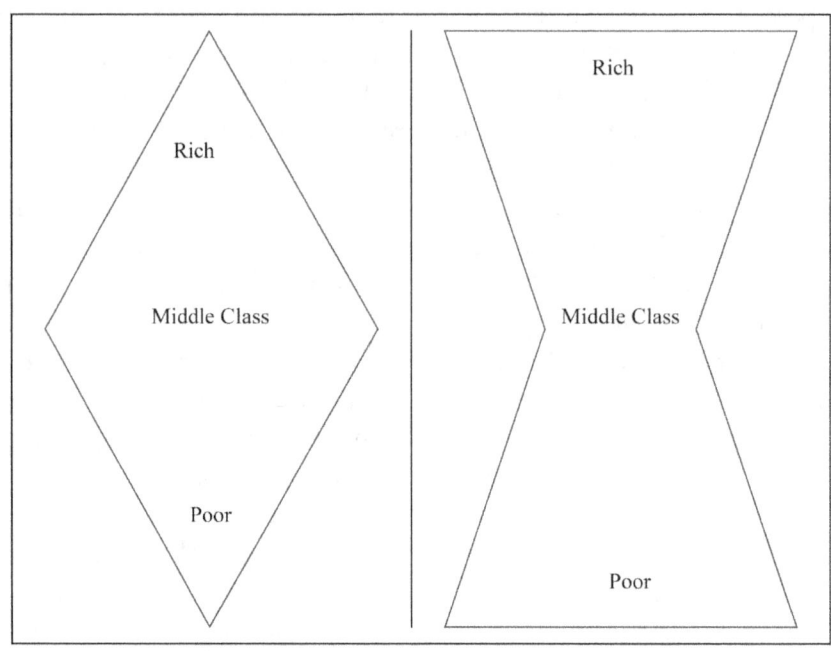

| Yesterday | Today |

'The Middle Class in a tight squeeze'

A few more people facing the brunt of being the middle class:

Better Off?

Recessions often depress middle-class moods along with incomes. Below, a sampling of middle-class folks from Lancaster, Pa., on what worries them about the current state of the economy and their fortunes. Click to see chart

Stay-at-home mom, married with two kids
She worries Democrats will raise taxes. "If people are hard up now it's only going to get worse."

Pastor, First Presbyterian Church
"Five years ago, I could dream big dreams... I can't be a dreamer at the moment."

Retired
"I feel sorry for young people today – the cost of living now is so much higher."

Unable to work
I fought like hell to get on disability" after a series of major heart problems. "Health care is the No. 1 issue."

Office manager of a software company
"I would really love to be retired," but her income supplements her husband's pension. "I'm just going to keep working."

General Manager, Graybills Tool and Die
He and his wife lost nearly $120,000 to a fraudulent mortgage lender. "I thought I was going to have a heart attack."

Not so long ago, being middle class meant a lot. It meant a reliable job with a considerable good pay, a home, access to health care, good education for children and a dignified retired life. But today, everything is uncertain and the standard of living is insecure. There is tremendous pressure on the existing middle class and those striving to achieve the levels of being in the middle class feel their chances are waning rapidly.

STATISTICS MAKES THE POINT CLEAR

- Just 38% of self-identified middle-class households say they live comfortably.
- 79% of Americans – and 78% of the middle class – say it is more difficult now than five years ago for people in the middle class to maintain their standard of living. (Fig 1)
- 72% of Americans say that they are less secure economically now than 10 years ago, while 47% of Americans are concerned about their personal economic security.

- 605,000 American jobs have been lost since the beginning of 2008 and the unemployment rate stood at 6.1% (9.4 million people unemployed) in August 2008.
- The economic cycle that began in 2000 and ended in 2008 was one of the weakest on record. The median income of working age households was $2,010 below its 2000 level.
- Approximately 66% of total income gains since 2002 have accrued to the top 10% of households.
- More than half of US-owned manufacturing production is now based in foreign countries due to outsourcing of jobs.
- The number of Americans living in poverty increased by 5.7 million between 2000 and 2007 to 37.3 million.
- 45.7 million Americans are currently without health insurance compared to 38.7 million in 2000. Members of the middle class are increasingly joining the ranks of the uninsured and under-insured
- People, especially the middle and lower middle class are going without needed coverage because healthcare is simply too expensive.
- Healthcare premiums have increased 78% since 2001.
- 60% of US companies offered their workers health insurance in 2007, down from 69% in 2000. (Fig 3)
- 20% of Americans say they have had difficulty paying other bills in the past five years because of medical bills.
- Studies show that soaring healthcare leads to bankruptcy in the middle class families.
- 1 in 33 Americans are expected to lose their homes to foreclosures over the next several years over subprime loans. (Fig 2)
- Middle class homeowners are increasingly cashing out the equity in their homes just to meet basic living expenses. Households cashed out $715 billion worth of home equity between 2001 and 2005.
- The Federal government provides no support to middle income families to afford preschool and only a few states offer universal preschool. This makes it harder for middle class families to balance work with parental responsibilities.

- Two out of three college graduates begin their careers with student loan debt, amounting to $19,300 for the median borrower.
- 46 million private sector employees in the US do not have a single paid sick day at work, while 86 million workers do not have paid leave to care for their sick children or dependent adults.
- 23% of private sector workers do not have any paid vacation at all.
- In 2007, one out of three American workers said the have not saved at all for their retirement, while in 2000, 78% of Americans said that they have saved at least some money for retirement.
- Prices of essential commodities have gone up tremendously. 4 dozen eggs, which cost $6.25 in 2000, now cost $9.61, an increase of 53.9%.
- Americans carry a record $956.9 billion in revolving debt by April 2008, an increase of 70% from a decade earlier.
- America's personal savings rate dipped into negative in 2005 for the first time since the Great Depression, and has not risen above 1% of income since then.
- We are in the middle of an unprecedented explosion inwhat might be considered a 'world middle class', which we define as those with incomes between $6,000 and $30,000 in PPP terms. And global income distribution is getting narrower, not wider.

Over the last ten years, we have already seen unprecedented expansion in the global middle class. But the pace of expansion here is likely to pick up much further still, reaching its peak in about a decade. As a result, an astonishing two billion people could join the global middle class by 2030! At around 30% of the world's population, this dwarfs even the 19th-century middle class explosion in its global scale.

* The BRICs [Brazil, Russia, India, China] continue to emerge as dominant forces in the global economy going forward. Our latest projections show the BRICs as four of the five largest economies in 2050.

* The rise of the N-11 [Next 11, The <u>Next Eleven</u> are eleven countries — Bangladesh, Egypt, Indonesia, Iran, Mexico, Nigeria, Pakistan, The Philippines, South Korea, Turkey, and Vietnam — identified by Goldman Sachs investment bank as having a high potential of becoming the world's largest economies in the 21st century along with the BRICs.] also remains a significant feature. The updated projections have resulted in somewhat higher GDP and income levels in a few decades time for some countries (Turkey, Philippines, Iran), and somewhat lower for others (Vietnam, Mexico, Korea). But the broad picture confirms our earlier work and ten of the N-11 are in the top twenty largest economies by 2050.

Like the BRICs 'dream' that we set out in 2003, there is nothing inevitable about the path for the Expanding Middle or the global projections that we set out here. The underlying assumptions we are making could clearly turn out to be wrong for a host of reasons. The advantage of setting out a framework is that it allows us to consider the plausibility of a broad range of alternative paths. We think that the more we and our clients understand the forces that are driving the Expanding Middle, the market opportunities that they present and the challenges they could present to businesses and policymakers, the better they will prepare themselves for the way that the world is changing.

While the total population of the planet will increase by about 1 billion people in the next 12 years, the ranks of the middle class will swell by as many as 1.8 billion. Of these new members of the middle class, 600 million will be in China. Homi Kharas, a researcher at the Brookings Institution, estimates that by 2020 the world's middle class will grow to include a staggering 52 percent of the global population, up from 30 percent now. The middle class will almost double in the poor countries where sustained economic growth is lifting people above the poverty line fast. For example, by 2025, China will have the world's largest middle class, while India's will be 10 times larger than it is today.

In 2005, China added as much electricity generation as Britain produces in a year. In 2006, it added as much as France's total supply. Yet, millions in China still lack reliable access to electricity; in India, more than 400 million don't have power. The demand in India will grow fivefold in the next 25 years. The World Tourism Organization estimates that outbound tourists will grow from today's 846 million a year to 1.6 billion in 2020.The statistics refer that in the United States the middle class is under tremendous pressure and is slowly disappearing. In the next few decades, one who still wants to be in the middle class may have to look forward to living in China or India. Unlike Western nations, these countries are helping the middle class to grow. In the US the middle class will ultimately have to choose between being rich and being poor, and the market economics will pay a bigger and bigger role in deciding who gets rich and who becomes poor.

The financial IQ of the Americans will be put to test: how to handle personal finances, where to invest and when to invest, et al. The better your understanding of the financial situation, the better off you will be. And since the US keeps printing paper money and keeps devaluating the dollar, the economics might not be as simple as increase in savings or hoard money. In fact, the more you hoard money, the worse off you may be in the future, because, the financial situation is not plagued by less money, but more dollars in circulation and a rising debt.

Causes of the Economic Crisis

To fully understand the factors that acted together in putting pressure on the middle class and gradually paving the path for the US to transform into a two-tier society, certain factors needs to be understood along with the economic ramifications of each of them. Most of these factors are interrelated and cannot act without the occurrence of the other and vice versa. Any of these factors, only by themselves, may not be responsible to the shrinking of the middle class, but all put together, becomes a deadly combination. And only through a proper understanding of these issues, can a person be prepared to face the situation as they exist. It does not take an economist to understand that the situation is going to get worse. A lot worse, in fact. For a common man, when wages go down while prices of petroleum and other essential commodities go up, it is a bad signal. And people are starting to understand that they cannot expect the politicians to save them from such a crisis. They will have to act themselves.

BABY BOOMER NOW RETIRING

The first of approximately 75 million baby boomers are turning 65; that is, the first of the baby boomers are started to retire in early 2007. This is the generation that has contributed fully to Social Security and Medicare. But the money that they have contributed is no longer there. Ideally, this money should have been invested and made available when the baby boomers retire. However, in US, this source of funds have been loaned to the government to finance increased deficit financing.

Since these baby boomers have contributed fully, they will have to be paid back. But if each one of them, of the 75 million baby boomers, starts to collect even $1,000 per month in Social Security and Medicare, it comes to $75 billion in additional monthly spending for the US government per month. This amount is similar to one Iraq war – every month. Now the big question is: Where will this money come from? The US government will go in to the red trying to meet this amount promised by their predecessors. The ability of the government to support the baby boomers, post retirement, will be tested. Either the retirement payments for baby boomers will have to cut drastically, or the present generation will have to be taxed heavily. Another option is the baby boomers will have to work longer than the retirement period of 65 years. But that would be just postponing the crisis situation for some more time. The government cannot change the fact that today, or tomorrow, the baby boomers are going to retire.

During the peak of their career, that is, when the baby boomers were between the age group of 30 to 40, they invested heavily into assets, stocks, mutual funds, etc. After their retirement, they will not be expected to keep on investing. They will be expected to cash in. That will create a greater supply situation in the market, which will in turn reduce the demand. So a stock market crash is not out of the question. However, not all of the baby boomers will cash in at the same time. Still a situation of excess supply in the stock market cannot be completely ruled out. As a more logical scenario, there may not be a sudden and volatile change in the stock market, but gradual slackening in demand without anything to reduce the supply will bring down the stock market after the baby boomers retire.

And we do not need any forecasts to make the scene gloomy. Baby boomers are in gloom already. The Wall Street crash, destroying $2 trillion in retirement savings, has left the baby boomers gasping for breath. With such a setback, the baby boomers will not be able to invest in real estate and it makes the scenario for hosing markets to raise a much difficult proposition. The 79 million boomers who have driven up the housing demand will be responsible for a reversal in the trend. There will be a huge difference in demand and supply. The supply is expected to supersede demand by three times. However, it is not only a problem with the US. One of the important trends that the world is facing now is regarding shifting demographics – specifically the general aging of the global population and the age of baby boomers. As the size of the workforce is projected to shrink in the future to a considerable extent such as in economies such as Japan, as mentioned earlier, the ability to support retirees under the current retirement system will be severely tested. More specifically, the baby boomers will have to work longer. This is going to be the most popular choice, as the advent of the knowledge economy has made baby boomers much more employable in their old age mostly due to their experience. However, we must also consider that baby boomers have already entered the age-group of 60 to 65: So, how much longer do baby boomers have to work to ensure a stable retirement maintaining the same lifestyle that they had before in the face of rising inflation, job losses and with the dollar dropping in value. Another question that will be very important in this regard is, how many baby boomers have saved enough for a better life in the future.

McKinsey's report on baby boomers provides a clear picture about what baby boomers will need to do in order to maintain a respectable post retirement without cutting down drastically on their standard of living.

These are some of the points to be noted from the study:

- The first baby boomer started receiving his/her social security payments last year at age 62. With the oldest baby boomer, now at age 63, there is not much time to lose from a personal as well as a social standpoint.

- Baby boomers will have to catch up with the society and will have to pay back to the society, to a certain extent, as they have consumed more and saved less than the previous generation when the market was booming.
- The most important problem, however, is not just savings, but savings at an accelerated rate. Households generally save at an accelerating rate with the highest rate of savings at the peak of their careers which normally extends from the age of 30 to the age of 50. However, this has not been the case for baby boomers in the US. Rather than saving at an accelerated rate, the baby boomers have been responsible for the collapse in the US savings rate from more than 10% in the mid 1980s to around 0% in the present situation.
- Taking into consideration that baby boomers will need 80% of their peak pre-retirement savings to sustain their retirement, McKinsey's report mentioned that about tho thirds of the baby boomer in the US are still not prepared for retirement. This result was drawn taking into account personal savings, socials security benefits, credit card balances, loans and other debts. Therefore according to McKinsey's report, about 69% of baby boomers are not prepared for retirement.
- Since baby boomers had scored woefully on the savings part in their pre-retirement period, McKinsey concluded that the best solution would be for baby boomers to work longer. This would not only help the US economy, as the government would not have to increase their burden of debt by borrowing money from the Fed to continue to grow at a decent rate, but would also allow baby boomers to save more.

To quote McKinsey:
If the Boomers stay on their current savings path, we project that Early Boomers [those aged 54 to 63 today] will begin drawing down their savings at an average of 65. But they could choose another path. They could postpone retirement, keep working, and use the additional income to increase their assets. By working longer, the Early Boomers would begin drawing down

their assets later, at an average age of 70 instead of 65. Such an additional accumulation of savings would have a significant impact on the shares of prepared and unprepared households. If Early Boomers were to draw down only their net financial assets, the share of prepared households almost doubles from 31 to 60 percent; if households also tap their home equity, the share of prepared households rise even more, from 38 to 69 percent.

However, it should be noted that McKinsey's study was released before the current financial crisis hit in its full force, asset prices crashed and before the real inflation went through the roof. Therefore, as is pointed out in the report that baby boomers can work still and increase their present savings, might be a dicey proposition. Hitherto, the US median housing price has already declined by more than 20% from the peak. In addition, McKinsey's study was done based on the amount of assets held by baby boomers in 2006. Since that time, the value of baby boomers' assets has declined from 15% to 20%.

THE FALL OF THE U.S. DOLLAR AND THE RISE OF DEBT

The fall of the dollar and the huge debts accumulated by the US are closely related. The dollar fell when President Richard Nixon took the US off the gold standard and converted into currency. The dollar is still falling and debt rising. Nixon made it sure that the US dictates the terms of world trade. The world wanted to do business with the US and had to accept the dollar as gold.

After President Nixon left, the US economy went into a slump till President Ronald Reagan came and started borrowing money coupled with cutting taxes. This started to increase the national debt and America started to borrow money to spend it and as a result boosting the economy. The economy saw a boom till 2000.

After 9/11 the US economy saw change. The US lowered interest rates and to compensate the gap, began printing more money. In 2003 and 2004, the Bank of Japan printed 35 trillion yen to save to dollar. That loan of $320 billion on the US kept interest rates low, which in turn kept the economy in good spirits as it was easy money from cheap debts. The interest rates, kept low, are now beginning to rise; they will have to be paid back.

On the other hand, the economy is slowing down. The mounting debt and slowing economy are like two different currents flowing in two opposite directions. When they come in contact with each other, the effect would be cataclysmic. US economy will crash. Due to the rising debt, the world economy is choking on US dollars. China ships products to the US and in turn US ships dollars to them. To keep the yuan from going up, the Chinese do not spend those dollars in the open market. Instead, they buy US assets, especially bonds, which keeps the prices of these bonds low. The low interest rate, encourage Americans to borrow and spend more money, in turn, shooting up the stock market and real estate prices. The Chinese use the US debt to collateralize their own debt and buy natural resources all over the world such as in Canada and Australia, booming up the markets in these places. But this boom is based on the debt accumulated by the US.

Therefore the problem is not shortage of money, buy too much of money. Since US bonds play a big part in the whole process, the country can easily raise the interest rate on their bonds and the problem may solve. However, because of the subprime crisis, the Fed cannot simply raise or lower interest rates. The US will have to keep interest rates low to save the domestic economy.

Thus, if the Fed tries to save the domestic economy, the international economy will pound the US by dumping dollars. On the other hand, if Fed tries to save the dollar internationally by raising the interest rates, the move will kill the domestic economy.

The dollar has been rallying pretty well recently and markets looked bearish. What this actually means is the bear market rally is coming to its fag end. And as the recession becomes more and more acute, it decreases the chances of the Fed to raise interest rates. And, at the same time, the real dollar interest rate being in the negative, a person would earn less interest income on a dollar deposit than the rate of inflation. This means that the person will not hold liquid money.

Although a strong dollar policy is always on the cards of the US policy makers, the Federal Reserve's focus is to revive the economy without any priority to strengthen the purchasing power of the dollar. According to US Treasury department, the national debt has grown more than $500 billion each year since 2003.

Now the question may arise as to how do the government managed to accumulate so much of debt. The debt is an accumulation of the budget deficits. The government in order to boost up spending has cut down on taxes for a long time now. Though in the short run the economy does benefit from deficit spending, however, those who hold the debt would want larger interest rates to compensate for their risk. Such a condition forces a government to keep debt under control.

As explained earlier, foreign countries, like China and Japan, have been increasing their holdings of Treasury bonds, keeping interest rates low. Many of these foreign holders of US debt are investing more in their own economies. Over time, as the demand for these bonds decrease, the interest rates will go up slowing down the economy. This low demand will also put pressure n the dollar to go down. As dollars and Treasury Securities becomes less desirable, their value will o down. As dollar comes down, foreign folders get paid back in currency that has gone down to a large extent. This increases the desirability and further decreases the demand on a continuous looping effect.

Even the US system of creating money actually results in amassing debts. When the US government decides to get money, it asks the Federal Reserve to buy bonds of the same amount from the government. For example, if the government wants $2 trillion, the Fed supplies this amount to the government by buying bonds worth that amount from the government. So the government generates Treasury bonds and putting a value on the bonds to the sum of $2 trillion hands them over to the Fed. Now it is the turn of the Fed to draw up $2 trillion in money, which is called Federal Reserve Notes. The Fed then takes these notes and trades them for the bonds. After the transaction is complete, the government takes the $2 trillion in Federal Reserve Notes and deposits the amount in a bank account, turning the paper notes into legal tender money adding $2 trillion to the money supply of the US.

It would be amazing to note that only 3% of the money supply of the US exists in physical currency. The other 97% of this money is digitized, which means that the money exists only in the computers. Now, bonds are instruments of debt. When the government issues bonds, it is indebted to pay that amount. When the Fed purchases these bonds with the money that it creates, the government is actually indebted to the Fed by that amount, which means that the government is promising to pay back that money to the Fed. In other words, the complete amount was created out of debt.

Now when this $2 trillion is deposited with the bank, the institution will keep 10% of the money as reserves and lend out the rest 90% ($180 billion). This $180 billion will again be deposited in bank/s and holding 10%, the bank/s will lend out the rest. That is how banks create money.

It would be logical to assume that the $180 billion is a part of the existing $200 billion deposit. However, the $200 billion is simply created out of thin air on top of the existing $180 billion deposit. Thais is the way money supply is expanded. This deposit creation loan cycle can go on till infinity. However, it is generally accepted that about $90 billion can be created on top of the original $2 trillion. In other words, for every x amount deposited with the banks, the banking system acting as a singular institute creates about 9 times i.e. 9x of the original deposit.

However, the question that may come to mind is: What is the basis of value on which the money is created. In other words, what is it that actually gives this newly created money value? That value is the money that is in circulation, in the pockets of people, in their bank accounts, money that has not yet been received. The new money 'steals' its value from the existing money supply in the economy; its value is taken from the same money everyone is holding.

Therefore, the total pool of money is being expanded in respective to the demand for goods and services. This infusion of money created out of this air, in turn, pushes up the equilibrium level of the demand and supply in the society. In other words, supply and demand finds equilibrium prices for the goods and services; this equilibrium level rise due to the infusion of money and diminishes the purchasing power of the dollars. This is generally referred to as inflation, which is nothing but a hidden tax on the public. So the government borrows money and the public pays the price for them.

This function of monetary expansion is inherently inflationary as only the money part is being expanded, without there being a proportional expansion of the goods and services in the economy. This complete process brings down the value of the currency of a country. For example, the value of one dollar in 1913 is exactly the same as 20 to 60 dollars in 2007. That is 96% devaluation in 94 years since the Fed came into existence.

Thus, in fine, in our financial system, money is debt and debt is money. The trend of money supply in US matches the trend of US national debt. Both are consistently upward rising curves. Both money and debt are directly proportional to each other. More the money, more the debt; and vice versa. Thus the only way money can be created in our economy is through loans, as every single existing dollar is owed to someone, by someone. This actually means that if everyone clears his/ her debt, including the government, there will not be a single dollar in circulation.

In 1835 America's national debt was completely paid off under President Andrew Jackson. Jackson's entire political campaign revolved around clearing the debt and shutting down the central bank. However, his dream was short lived and America succeeded to install another Central Bank in 1913 – the Federal Reserve – the institution that guarantees that America will perpetually be in debt.

Therefore, money is created out of debt, which transforms into loans which are based on the bank's reserves backed by deposits. Over that is the banking system where any deposit creates nine times its original value in turn debasing the money supply and raising the prices in the economy. Since all this money is created out of debt and circulated randomly, people become detached from the original debt and a disequilibrium results where people are forced to compete for cheap labor in order to pull up enough money from the money supply to cover their cost of living, which has now gone up due to the inflationary forces as there is more money in circulation in the economy. That is the reason why the middle class is being squeezed to the maximum, trying to get money to cover their cost of living.

When a person borrows money, it has to be paid back with interest. In other words, the money that the banks lend out will have to be returned to them with the interest paid as well. But if money is borrowed from a Central Bank and is expanded by commercial banks, through loans, only the principal is the money supply. So where is the money for the interests going to come from?

There is no source for that. The ramifications of this fact are staggering as the amount of money owed back to the banks always exceeds the amount that is available. This is the reason for the constant inflation in the economy, because, new money will always be required to cover up the deficit that is existing in the economy. But new money also means new debts and the whole process comes in a circle. It also means that bankruptcies will be there and is built in to the system. It means that there will always be poor pockets in the society.

If a person is unable to pay his/her mortgage, the banks will take away the property. But such a situation is inevitable due to the faulty system and it is enraging as the money the banks loan out did not even legally exist in the first place. Every time a person borrows money from the bank, whether it be mortgage loan or credit card, or to start a business; the money given out is not only counterfeit, but is an illegitimate form of consideration. The bank never had the money as the property on the first place to begin with. This is the main reason for the dollar to keep dropping, the reason why middle class Americans are being squeezed.

GAP INCREASING BETWEEN THE RICH AND THE POOR

The inherent fallacy of modern economics is that the rich get richer and poor get poorer. Money attracts money and as the economic model we follow generates money out of nothing, it always tends to tilt towards those who have money. The rich gets richer, even in a bad economy.

The world, as it stands today on a mountain of debt, will continue to inflate. This means high inflation with prices going up continuously. This may result in hyperinflation and life will become very difficult for those down the rungs of the ladder. Because whatever they earn would not be sufficient to feed them as the inflationary process will keep prices out of their reach and unemployment will ensure low income prevailing in most poor houses. Not only will fuel costs go up, so will the cost of food. As the dollar keeps dropping on its value, countries like India and China will import more food from the United States as the terms of trade will tilt in their favor. Fighting wars also costs money. For example, the US used to spend $500,000 per minute on the Iraq war. At the same time, President Bush vetoed health insurance coverage for children.

So, the government is will to spend on wars rather than taking care of their children. Having said that the problem in our present economy exists not because there is less money, but because there is too much money; it should be pointed out that excess money means most workers will have to work harder but earn lesser. This is again because the currencies of the world, including the dollar, are becoming less and less valuable. Even if the pay of a worker rises, the decline of the purchasing power of money will more than negate the boost. Increase in the price of oil, decrease in the value of homes, increase of taxes and decrease in the value of stocks will contribute to the squeezing of the poor.

Lets compare the rise in income to the rise in gold. A decade ago, old was about $275 an ounce, while today the price of gold has gone up to a whopping $700 an ounce. Keeping in parity, people's income should have gone up by 250% just to keep up with the loss of purchasing power of the dollar. Oil has gone up by 800%. Did your income go up by 800%? Otherwise how will you buy oil without reducing the consumption of it? There will be people whose income has jumped 800% and more. But they will be few in number. And for those, whose income has not gone up to that extent, are technically in a state of personal recession, with no way out.

Let us take an example as per the research brief issued on July 1996 by the Public Policy Institute of California under the head "Income Gap Between rich and Poor Widening in California":

Income inequality—a measure of how the income pie is divided among all members of society—has increased dramatically in the United States over the past 30 years. To determine whether California trends mirrored those of the nation, Deborah Reed, Melissa Glenn Haber, and Laura Mameesh analyzed annual changes in income distribution from the late 1960s through 1994. Using five measures of inequality, 26 definitions of income, and two data series (the Current Population Survey and the Census), the researchers compared income levels and trends in California with national and regional levels and trends. Their findings, presented in *The Distribution of Income in California*, provide the most comprehensive picture ever assembled on income inequality in California.

Inequality growing faster in California- At both the state and national levels, the widening income gap results from real earnings growth at the top of the income range and an absolute decline at the bottom. Until the late 1980s, the trends in the state and the nation were remarkably similar. However in 1987, income inequality began to expand more rapidly in California—not because the rich have grown richer in California than in the rest of the nation, but because, as a group, the poor have become poorer.

The expanding gap between rich and poor in California is further highlighted by comparing the trendlines with those of other states. In 1969, 20 states had higher household income inequality and male earnings inequality. By 1989, only five states had higher household income inequality, and only two had higher male earnings inequality.

Household income- As shown in Figure 1, household income inequality was similar for California and the nation in most of the years studied, fluctuating in the 1970s and advancing strongly since then. In both the state and the nation, inequality increased more rapidly during economic recessions. However, the recessions of the early 1970s and 1990s hit California much harder than the nation as a whole as reflected in the larger increases in inequality.

Annual earnings of male workers-Labor income is the largest component of household income and, as might be expected, revealed many of the same patterns as household income over the past 30 years. It is important to look at both measures of inequality because trends in household inequality are complicated by changes in family size and marriage behavior. In contrast, labor income inequality measures the disparity of income among individuals rather than families and is not directly affected by changes in household structure.

Although household income may be a better indicator of general economic well-being, labor income provides a clearer picture of changes in the economy. Figure 2 shows how much the distribution of annual earnings has widened among male workers in California.

The middle trend line of the graph shows the percentage change in real, inflation-adjusted median male earnings since 1967. The lower line shows the decline of male earnings at the 20th percentile, the income level that separates the bottom 20 percent of earners from the top 80 percent. The upper line shows earnings at the 80th percentile.

As reflected in the figure, median male earnings fell 20 percent between 1967 and 1994. This 20 percent decline represents a drop in median male earnings from $31,252 to $25,000 in real 1994 dollars.

At the 20th percentile, male earnings fell 40 percent from $17,316 in 1967 to $10,400 in 1994. In 1967, a man at the 80th percentile earned $44,345, about two and a half times what a man at the 20th percentile earned. By 1994, male earnings at the 80th percentile had increased 13 percent to $50,000, about five times what a man at the 20th percentile earned in that year.

This comparison of earnings of men in the upper-middle to the lower-middle of the distribution is one measure of inequality. By this measure, male earnings inequality increased by 88 percent between 1967 and 1994.

CONSIDERING THE IMPLICATIONS

Income inequality is particularly disturbing when it is fueled by a decline in the income of poor individuals and households. This is the pattern that has characterized the increasing inequality in California over the past three decades.

It is important to note, however, that the results of this study do not indicate that people who were poor in the past have necessarily gotten poorer. The data for this analysis are cross-sectional (snapshots of those in income groups in each year) not longitudinal, and therefore do not follow the fortunes of specific families or individuals over time. What the analysis does tell us is that the poor in 1994 were considerably worse off than the poor in 1967. Moreover, as income falls at the bottom of the distribution, a greater percentage of people fall below the official poverty line. In other words, more Californians are poor today than were poor in the late 1960s.

The distribution of income across a population is relevant to many policy domains, including economic development, tax and transfer programs, public sector employment, education and training, and workforce productivity. To develop policies that can promote equity and opportunity, as well as efficiency, in the California economy, legislators and other public officials need to understand the forces underlying the state's growing inequality. In a follow-up study, the institute's researchers will identify these forces and assess their relative effects on income distribution in California.

According to the report of Organization for Economic Cooperation and Development released in AP: The United States has the highest inequality and poverty in the OECD after Mexico and Turkey, and the gap has increased rapidly since 2000, the report said. France, meanwhile, has seen inequalities fall in the past 20 years as poorer workers are better paid. OECD Secretary-General Angel Gurria said that the study, which took three years to complete, would be useful to policymakers because it is coming out just as the world is undergoing "the worst crisis in decades."

And these are not the only reasons why the poor are getting poorer and thr rich are getting richer. Let us take for example what the US government did to bail out its rich friends Fannie Mae and Freddie Mac. When corporates like these die, they turn to their best pals, the US government to bail them out of the crisis and in the process pocket money by depriving the poor. The government appeals to the patriotism of the American people to bail out their rich friends. The richest of the rich use the system to legally steal from the American people by calling for the sense of patriotism. Baling out "institutions that stands for American superiority" actually translates to "helping out rich friends". Such bail outs can mean a lot of things. The US government has to print money and take more debts to bail out giants such as Fannie, Freddie, Merrill, Lehman and AIG. This leads to higher inflation hitting the poor under the belt. Rather than protecting people, by joining hands with the rich friends and making them richer, the US government is making life for the poor and the middle class ore expensive. In other words, the rich are getting richer at the expense of the poor and the middle class. The US government protects its rich and incompetent friends. Generally if a business fails, it fails. But if a business is rich and the businessman is politically connected, then the business grows richer. The irony is, when people start getting poor, the look up to the government to help them out; the same government that made them poor.

According to a New York Times article released in 2005:

- 2005 has seen great disparity between the rich and the poor. Data for this year shows that income for the richest, approximately 1 percent of Americans with incomes that of more than $348,000 per year, received the largest share of national income since 1928. So the US government stuffed their pockets with dollars this year. Even those people existing in the top 10 percent of American population earning roughly $100,000, reached income share that had not been seen before the Great Depression.

- The total income reported in the US increased 9 percent in 2005. However, average income for the people in the bottom 90 percent dipped .06 percent from 2004.
- The gains of the economy were largely accrued to the top 1 percent of the US population. Their income rose to an average of more than $1.1 million each, an increase of about 14 percent.
- The collective income of the top 300,000 Americans were almost equal to the collective income of the bottom 150 million Americans. On individual basis, per person the richest group got 440 times as much as the average person in lower rungs of the society earned. This gap is almost double than the gap that that existed in 1980.
- The Internal Revenue Service estimates that it is able to accurately tax 99 percent of wage income, which is equal only to about 70 percent of business. Most of the unreported and underreported income flows to the few upper echelons with the highest wealth.

In capitalism, it is the middle class who has always been the source of taxation. Neither the poor, nor the rich, pay taxes. The poor cannot pay taxes while the rich have too much of money to pay taxes.

According to Treasury Secretary Henry M. Paulson Jr.:

Such a large share of the income gains are going to the very top, at a minimum, raises serious questions about continuing to provide tax cuts averaging over $150,000 a year to people making more than a million dollars a year, while saying we do not have enough money. The rapid pace of technological change has been a major driver in the decades-long widening of the income gap in the United States.

Jobs Being Exported (CHINDIA)

As internet became available in countries such as India and China, life in US became cheaper. Cheaper for a few industrialists though, while, on the other hand, the middle class was hit with a brick stick. Industrialists found out that cheap labour was available in these countries and they can be used to do various jobs at as much as 10 times lesser money than the existent rate in the US. Thus started outsourcing. As more and more jobs started to drain out of the US, there were deep concerns in the economy about how to control such drain. Industrialists argued that Americans will find enough jobs in the highly changing technological environment. However, a couple of decades later, America realize that outsourcing doe not only take jobs away from the US citizens, it hurts the economy.

- According to the Economic Policy Institute, more than 3 million jobs have been lost due to outsourcing since 1998 in the manufacturing segment alone. The US manufacturing trade deficit played a significant role in this regard.
- According to Goldman Sachs, about half of the total job loss in the US has been in the information and in the services sector. The amount comes to 400,000 to 600,000 jobs in the information and services segment alone.
- According to Deloitte Research, one-third of all the major financial institutions in the US are sending work offshore, with 75 percent of them reporting they would do so within the next 24 months.
- Boom in the software industry in India, China and other South East Asian countries would not have occurred if not for outsourced jobs from the US. The hardest hit segment is information technology. According to Global Insight, the US lost 104,000 information technology jobs to offshore outsourcing between 2000 and 2003.
- According to The Economic Policy Institute, employment in the US software-producing industries fell by 128,000 jobs between 2000 and 2004. About 100,000 new jobs producing software for export to the US, supporting the

US companies, were created in India over the same period of time.

- According to INPUT Research, projects outsourcing of state and local government technology contracts in the public sector, will grow from $10 billion last year to $23 billion till the end of 2009.
- According to the estimates of The Economic Policy Institute, between 1993 and 2000, due to trade policies unfavorable to US and increase in the U.S. trade deficit, Americans lost a net 3 million jobs and possible job opportunities due to high wage rates. The growth in the NAFTA trade deficit is associated with nearly 900,000 lost jobs and through 2002
- According to Forrester Research, U.S. employers will move 3.4 million white-collar jobs and $136 billion in wages overseas by 2015. According to a University of California at Berkeley, 14 million jobs are at risk of being sent offshore, and predict job losses will exceed the Forrester study's projections.
- According to the estimates of Gartner, 10 percent of computer services and software jobs will be moved overseas by the end of 2009.
- According to a survey by Deloitte Research, the world's 100 largest financial services firms expect to shift $356 billion worth of its operations and about two million jobs to low-wage countries such as China and India over the next five years.

Ironically, this situation where we are today, would not have risen, but for the technological strides made by the US and the telecom and communications bubble burst. The corporates took advantage of a world, better communicated than a decade back and grabbed the opportunity to ship jobs to countries with lower wage rate, so they can make more profits. Estimated 400,000-500,000 jobs per year are being exported to cheap overseas labor markets. Due to the internet, manufacturers are not pressed for setting up offshore centres in these countries; instead, they are 'remotely' operating these centres. Remote operations means that a company can have people working for them in all the countries across the globe while the employer can sit in his chair and oversee the complete operations. Outsourcing is a creation of the digital world. And US is the pioneer of digitization.

However, as the statistics say, though web-based companies, telecom companies, companies providing back end operations and assistance in a business to business or a business to customer model, business process development companies, et al were the first ones to join the bandwagon, outsourcing is now expanded to cover and touch every segment of the economy including the public sector. So much so that outsourcing companies based out of US are approaching the Government to bag orders which they are outsourcing to other countries. The world is now connected by the World Wide Web and if you are in Massachusetts, and you want to know where the nearest Starbucks is located, you may be calling up someone sitting at Thiruvananthapuram in India for the information.

Though the immediate and short term result of the process of outsourcing is the loss of jobs in the US, the whole process has far-reaching effects and long-term consequences. Among other things, outsourcing is a drain of technology and knowledge base to other countries. People in other countries are also privy to the sociological secrets of the people of US because medical and financial records of the people are also being exported to other countries. Each time a company in the US transfer knowledge bases overseas, whether it be manufacturing or technology or research or back end operations, it is going to be a service that will be performed by a competing economy. It does not matter whether that economy is far below US, or whether that economy is just emerging, it is still a competing economy. It is a work that is not being done by the people of the US. The result is further pressure on the US economy – which is anyways reeling from pressures put on it by its own people.

The statistics mentioned above, shows that every job that replaces one that is outsourced out of the US, pays approximately 20 percent less than the job that was exported overseas. So we have a continuing downward pressure on the wages in this country, where people will now have to compete with their competitors abroad to bring in more profits for the company that they are working in. In other words, the savings that the companies are making due to outsourcing is going in to the pockets of the very few at the top of the ladder, while the working class is being hard pressed to maintain a living out of their reach with means that are below the market value. The whole system also has an impact on education because that money is not available to the tax base that pays for education. The whole process, in turn, diminishes the income-tax base for the federal government and state governments.

Free Trade is a concept devised by the capitalist. Now that same concept is hurting the US. Outsourcing increases this deficit. America's trade deficit now amounts to $4 trillion in external debt and the country has to borrow $3 billion, every day, to support this deficit. To top it all, the dollar is plummeting. And yet the government says, "Free trade is good."

America now depends on other countries for almost everything. From oil, clothes, food, electronics to even getting data about themselves. And other countries are taking advantage of this situation. One does not have to understand micro and macro economics to get the grasp of why outsourcing exists. It is a simple question of cheap solutions. Countries like India, China and Philippines are accepting orders at one tenth of what a company has to shell out if it wants to have the work done in the US. The great sense of US patriotism does not apply to the US companies. They will always look for cheaper alternatives which are readily available in developing economies. A US worker cannot work at one tenth of the market price. Therefore he loses his job to someone who is sitting in Philippines with a computer developed in US. The US policy makers mouths words like competitiveness, productivity, efficiency – while these high-sounding phrases are nothing but substitutes of one single phrase "cheap labor".

Many of US policy makers believe that outsourcing is a short-term problem needed for long-term economic well being. However, 28 years of trade deficit and mounting external debt due to imports, tells another tale. And the mounting debt will keep on mounting as more and more technology, jobs and information is outsourced.

In case people that that outsourcing can be counterbalanced with insourcing, they will be living in a fool's paradise. Insourcing means foreign direct investment in to the US. And the US cannot keep up with the Chinese as far as foreign direct investment is concerned. China has already surpassed the US in that regard. They do it with the bonds the bought from the US government itself. Foreign companies are not investing in US markets by setting up operations there – like what happened in the time of President Ronald Reagan. They are not contributing to the US economy. Instead, they are taking away jobs and increasing US debts because the nation has mindlessly opened its doors to the foreign countries under the banner of free trade.

Any country and any economy will have trade deficits. But the US has been borrowing money to support its consumption habits over 28 years. The fact is free trade is not going to bring any prosperity to the US unless a balance is stroked to eliminate deficits and maintain vigorous, healthy trade with the world. But such a situation requires a manufacturing base and reduction of dependency on foreign oil, clothing and a host of other goods and services. In other words, America should consume what it produces and not consume more than what it can produce by borrowing from other countries. Or at the least, should reduce its consumption of foreign goods.

According to a study by the Federal Reserve a few years ago, if US trade deficit rise beyond 5 percent of the nation's GDP, an inflection will be created which can result in a crisis. The US trade deficit is approaching 6 percent of GDP. This is the debt that the US borrows from countries abroad to support its imports. The tax base of the US can diminished to such an extent due to outsourcing that jobs will become so poor paying so as people will not be able to pay taxes.

The US needs to protect itself and get rid of the thought that free trade is good for them. The US government will have to stop destruction of jobs due to outsourcing. The American companies, based out of US and providing goods and services to the American people will have to stop killing jobs in their own country and send the jobs overseas. They can set up bases in other countries and continue trade, but not at the cost of American people. It can be done through government regulations or appealing to the conscience of the American corporate. But if the American companies refuse to pay heed, then government regulation might be a necessity.

However, silver lining in this gloomy scenario is that many jobs are coming back to the US especially in the software segment. This is because the US companies cannot just survive by cutting costs; they will also have to keep in mind the quality of the product. In many places the quality of work being done in other countries fall below the standards as those done by the Americans. Also there are hidden costs involved when companies outsource jobs.

Nevertheless, at a time when the US is facing serious economic problems and should get more jobs for its citizens, the companies are outsourcing huge chunks of jobs deepening the trade deficit even further. Increased trade with lower wages will increase income inequality. On an average, almost 20 percent increase in income inequality in the US is a direct result on exported jobs. Recent economic studies indicate that real wages have stagnated since 1973, notwithstanding the fact that productivity has increased rapidly. This is directly related to inflation and is inversely proportional to it. In other words, as inflation increases real wage goes down. And combined with job losses due to outsourcing, the future does not look too good for the American middle class.

Outsourcing also brings down the bargaining power of the workforce. As workers demand more, the companies just have to threaten them saying that if they do not work at their present wages, the jobs will be shifted overseas.

Coupled with this problem is the shrinking of wages for the American people. As per the latest Current Population Survey, in the US, there are now 24 million adult native-born Americans, between the age group of 18 to 64 years, who have no education beyond high school and who are either unemployed or not employed in the labor force.

Due to the severity of the economic downturn the US is facing, the long-term decrease in wages and that employment for the middle and the least educated is likely to go up.

This trend had been there for sometime. Since the last few decades, the share of these blue-collared Americans who have been working has been declining and their wages, after adjusting for inflation, have been falling too. On the other hand, immigrants in the labor market, has grown drastically. However, the problem cannot be seen in the light of labor shortage. If any labor shortage if at all existed, wages and employment rates should have gone up instead of gong down; something that has been happening for a long time.

If the recession is long and deep, which in all probabilities is going to be the case, America could see native-born workers migrating, settling and working for wages under working conditions that were previously unacceptable. That, in other words, mean a lot of people are going to go down on the quality of life that they were leading a couple of decades back.

The price of essential commodities such as milk, plane ticket and various other products escalated in 2008 at nearly the fastest pace in a generation and it is only the beginning. American middle class was not ready for this onslaught and it took away a bigger chunk from the buying power of the consumers.

As consumer prices rise due to shockwaves of recession hitting the economy, weekly wages fell .09 percent in June – the biggest drop in almost four years. Both these methods act together and contribute significantly towards the shrinking of the middle class as now they earn leaser money and will have to make a decision of whether to try and increase the amount of money for consumption and maintain the standard of living, or to go down the standard of living. In any case, the pressure on this class is evident, and any movement along the social ladder depends more on which age group the family belongs to. For example, if the family is between 25 to 50 years, they look forward to means to increase their standard of living and move up the ladder. But if they are in their retirement stage or in post retirement, then, most often than not they are not left with a choice but to go down. Because rising of consumer price coupled with decreasing wages and cut in pension plans can lend a deathblow to these people and some of them have to postpone their retirement indefinitely to and may still not catch up with these changes.

In the last ten years, American jobs went out of the United States at an ever-accelerating rate of speed. American workers stood in unemployment lines, while major corporations insourced, outsourced and offshored jobs to the emerging economies. They could obtain labor for $1.00 an hour and sometimes even lesser than that. As a result, many families dwelling in the middle class have gone down to becoming working poor.

While the government displaced American workers, it engaged millions of illegal alien workers in blue collar-jobs such as meatpacking, chicken, hotel, roofing, landscaping, processing, paving, construction and other trade jobs.

On one end, the government offered hundreds of thousands of H-1B and L-1 visas that displaced 890,000 American workers out of jobs while, on the other it is importing cheap labor from overseas. America's manufacturing base and the ability to sell products to the world has been constantly diminishing with the increase in the power of corporations and the Federal Reserve to control taxes, tariffs and commodities markets.

And it is a hell of a rich man's club, but it's turning America's Middle Class into the working poor class.

General Electric, that has built its empire on American soil, is now known as the father of outsourcing. It may be one of the best examples of how companies are using new technology to cut costs and outsource more. The company has, hitherto, outsourced 12,000 jobs to India. These workers provide back-end support to the company answering credit card inquires and giving IT technical assistance. They also handle network security for the company.

According to researchers, Bank of America, one of America's largest banks, eliminated 5,000 jobs while outsourcing 1,250 jobs to India. The bank has announced that it is going to cut another 12,000 jobs in the next two years. The employees of Bank of America were also given severance pay on condition they train their replacements.

Affiliated Computer Services has outsourced 1,300 jobs to India in the past three years. This company multiplied its profits by paying half the wage rate of that of America's.

Halliburton (incidentally this company was formerly run by former Vice President Dick Cheney as its CEO) enjoys 45 subsidiaries in offshore tax havens. Countries like India and China are hungry to see their economy rise. Thus they provide tax free zones and give huge tax benefits to companies such as these to set up bases away from the US. Halliburton is helping reconstruct Iraq with $73 million in equipment and services.

In March 2003, the Bank of New York run by Thomas Reny sent 250 computer software jobs to Mumbai where it already had a base and was employing 670 workers. It plans to open a software development center in the Philippines shortly.

American Telephone and Telegraph, or what was previously known as Ma Bell, outsourced 500 customer-service jobs to India in 2003. The company had outsourced another 3,000 jobs before.

US based Dell Computers, which employ 3,000 Indians in Bangalore and Hyderabad in India had cut 21,000 American jobs in 2001 and in 2003. These are only a few handful of the top corporations who believes in cutting cost at the cost of American citizens. However, if a company outsources job to other countries to save themselves money at the cost of fellow Americans, then the least one can expect from them is passing on at least a percentage of the money saved to its customers – especially when inflation is rising and things are getting too costly for a middle-class American. However, the additional savings goes into the pockets of the CEOs and CFOs and no benefits are passed on to the customers.

According to a study, Americans compete with 1.3 billion Chinese and 1.1 billion Indians whose medium income hovers around at $2,000 a year. People from these countries can afford to work for $5.00 a day; whereas, Americans must make at least $15.00 an hour to maintain a decent standard of living.

These statistics mean that America's middle class is on its way to the bottom of the standard of living strata as its jobs are outsourced, insourced and offshored. It means millions work lower the level to support their families without any ob security.

However, there are arguments that support outsourcing on the basis that it cuts down excess flack in the American economy and increase the productivity as well as competitiveness of the Americans. The argument still holds true that even if excess flab is there in the economy, it cannot exist with the middle class or in the middle class jobs. The excess flab is gathered by the top tier of the society while the middle class gets the brick bat.

There is also the argument that maybe if such jobs are not outsourced, consumer products will be out of reach of the middle class. However, the sort of jobs that are being outsourced has no bearing with the essential commodity prices which is rising continuously. They are jobs in the technology, software and back-end support which does not, at least directly, affect inflation.

And since such outsourcing does not affect goods of mass consumption, there is more to it than just outsourcing that is bringing down the standard of living of the middle class. If the US economy were based on the true cost of living, and not inflated my pumping in more and more money to fill the pockets of the richest segment, an average American's basic needs would not only be met, but the companies might not have the need at all to look beyond the shores of the US as prices would have been decided on true values and not inflated by the economy. Now America has to depend on foreign countries for anything and everything.

INFLATION OR DEFLATION?

Inflation is defined as an increase in the amount of currency in circulation, resulting in a relatively sharp and sudden fall in its value and rise in prices: it may be caused by an increase I the volume of paper money issued or of gold mined, or a relative increase in expenditures as and when the supply of goods fail to meet the demand.

The inflation as is faced by the US is however a result of an increase in the amount of money in circulation in the economy due to high debts, high borrowing and a fall in the value of the dollar as has been explained in the previous chapters.

Inflation hits the middle and the lower income class the most as prices of essential goods go up and the same salary that is drawn a decade back will not suffice to maintain the same lifestyle in present times. That is why companies raise salaries of people. But often the raise cannot match the rate of inflation and those is when the squeeze starts on the middle class as they either have to earn more and go up the ladder, or remain where they are and become poorer in the real terms.

Inflation took off in the American markets with the birth of the Federal Reserve, as the Fed is an instrument using which the government borrows money and creates inflation. Another important point in history with reference to inflation is when President Richard Nixon took America off the gold standard and made it into currency.

Hodges marks FDR's dollar devaluation against gold as the elimination of the gold standard. Figures 8 and 9 above illustrate the present condition of the US economy and to what extent inflation has shot up. Since 1971, there has been too much of US dollars in circulation. With huge debts, the credit creation by the banks has shot through the roof. Without a gold or silver standard, there is no check on the amount of money or credit that can be created and US has been creating money to the hilt.

The Federal Reserve has all the powers to control the supply of money and thus, control inflation. However, it has been refusing to do so since its inception. A stimulus in terms of money can be used in a productive way, or be used to fuel and meet consumption. The US seems to be more interested in consuming and the Federal reserve maintains no control over this critical outlet of inflation.

An abundance of money and credit in the economy badly distorts the fabric of the economy. Infusion of excess money has not been transformed into savings, earned income or more gains from production. In the US economy, this stimulus has fueled consumption, bubbles in stock and property; this in turn has distorted a healthy and growing economy. The problem is, there has been a bubble bursts in different segments of the economy, such as the real estate, and people who were millionaires has been turned into bankrupts. Credit is necessary for any economy to grow and a growing economy will always have fiscal and trade deficits. But as the saying goes: Too much of anything is bad; too much money and credit for too long a period will cripple the foundation of any economy.

After President Nixon decided to shift the US economy from the gold standards, the US and all other nations have possessed fiat money. The dollars' value comes from its acceptance as money by consumers and governments and is intrinsically worth only the paper on which it is printed. This removes the bar from printing as much money as the government wants. And that is what the US government had been doing

– printing money – and thereby amassing mountains of debt. A look at graphs 10 and 11 will show how extremely indebted US has become and why deficits have been the norm.

Both the figures on trade deficits and national debt shows that prior to the gold standard the US economy rarely suffered from deficits or debts, and after US was removed from gold standard, debt and deficits have become the trend. A fiat currency gradually increased the cost of living hurting the middle class. Also, such a huge deficit harms the business community. The fiat currency have fueled inflation and made American producers to compete with emerging nations. No wonder the US imports cheap goods from China to feed their population. These emerging nations offer cheaper labour and fewer regulations and thus American companies have closed shop in the US and moved them abroad, again, hurting the middle class by denying them job opportunities.

The inflation of the past 35 years has gradually destroyed the productive economy of the US and made it into a society that depends excessively on other nations to supply them with goods for consumption. And the icing on the cake is the falling value of the dollar. Since the world is choking on too many dollars, people and nations wants less and less of it. This is going to make the situation of deficit worse.

At present day, the US government has so much in debts that it comprises almost half of the US economy. As a result of increased borrowing and spending over a period of half a century, the average middle class family is overburdened with taxes, inflation, state fees and so on. On the other hand are raising costs of the essential items of leading a life such as food, healthcare and energy. Decade's back, when America was a superpower, the cost of living was far less as the real inflation was much lower than what it is today. Moreover, in the years to come, the trillions in medical care and social security obligations will render an even larger share of the pie of economy to the government. To fulfill its obligations the government may have to deny the middle class its basic necessities, or charge the existing working force exorbitant taxes.

It must also be noted that inflation creates its own vicious circle. Economic boom quickly transforms into bubbles as the money supply in an economy increases in order to take advantage of the boom. There are two ways in which a bubble burst occurs. One is through deflation, in which case the money supply contracts as investors and consumers default on debts and liquidate losses. The other way is through hyperinflation. More money is created, generally by the government, to keep the economy going and stave off the collapse of the economy and liquidation of credit and money. As debt piles up, the forces for a deflation grow stronger, as the government pushes in more and more money and credit to prevent deflation.

Furthermore, subsequent inflations followed by the first, need to be larger to match previous rounds of inflation. Eventually the hyperinflation reaches its peak when the currency has lost all its value and has come back to what it is – leaflets of paper – or when the government decides to back the currency with something tangible such as gold or silver which are the truest forms of money. The whole process is like blowing up a balloon. The air becomes the money supply in the economy and constant money supply constantly inflates the balloon. Eventually too much air causes a complete bursting of the balloon, in which the air becomes worthless – just like money. The US economy is now being inflated through constant money supply from the government. It is to be seen how much money it can support till a bubble burst occurs. Till that time, there will be inflation, and more inflation and the middle and the lower class will have to bear the brunt of it.

Inflation is fundamentally a man-made action and in the case of the US, inflation has been made by the Federal Reserve and the government. However, the end result is always deflation. Deflation can be prevented, but only through accelerated inflation. The question that comes to mind is whether American monetary policy favors deflation or hyperinflation.

However, the world has never stood in such a position before as it is standing today. Not only the US, but in other economies such as the UK, Canada, Europe and Australia money supply is growing. Money growth in countries such as China and India is twice the amount of that in other developed countries. This is because the emerging economies are hungry for growth. For the first time, almost every country is operating with fiat money, something that is not baked by assets such as gold and silver.

As you can see, from November 2008 through February 2009, gold rose from around $700 to nearly $1,250. This whole process is fundamentally dangerous as there is little or no protection against increasing the earnings by governments and central banks.

It also means that this whole empire is established on nothing and is not backed by anything that is of real value. Money, especially currency is of no real value unless it is backed by something other than confidence. Fundamentally, the various currencies of almost all the countries are the same.

The Dollar, Yen, Euro, and Yuan are all just pieces of paper that derive their value from public acceptance, government enforcement and they depend on each other's confidence when trade takes place between two countries. Governments and central banks play a tricky game of testing the confidence of the public and they keep on increasing and inflating their economy. The price of gold, silver and all commodities will explode due to hyperinflation in all currencies if and when the market decides there is too much money in the financial system.

By constantly increasing the credit and money supply, as is done in most economies, policy makers cannot stop, but can postpone the natural recession. However, it is widely admitted that a little recession is healthy and helpful for a growing economy. But only a little. Such a recession bolsters the entire system by cutting the flack in the economy and making the economy more productive with increased competitiveness of the players in the economy. Such a recession makes the economy stronger and prepares itself for subsequent expansion.

However, there is not much more room for the Federal Reserve to maneuver around or to postpone the recession without pushing the US economy into. Once hyperinflation strikes, the middle class will be on the verge of wiping out. Or in most cases they will go down the ladder and they will have to stay there till economy stabilizes again. On the other hand, if the Federal Reserve cannot contract the money supply in the economy as it would bring about the greatest deflation in recent history.

In the US, the total credit market debt as a percentage of GDP now exceeds that of 1929. And the irony is: In 1929, the US country was self sufficient in energy, manufacturing and capital. In the present world, the US imports most of its energy, while inflation has destroyed the manufacturing sector. And to top it, the US is history's greatest debtor.

Unfortunately, most Americans are not aware of the situation. They have been educated to believe that government involvement and the involvement of the of the central bank is a part of a free market economy. Lest of all the middle class is not aware how to save themselves or shield themselves from the onslaught of inflation that is going to befall the economy.

To avoid a deflationary depression, the US government will continue to create new money to monetize the mountains of debts and to keep economic activity from stagnating. In the coming years, to meet the entitlement demands such as those of retirement policies and all, and also to meet the budget gap, monetary expansion will keep on going at an accelerated rate.

The US government and the Federal Reserve have been deceiving the Americans as to the real level of inflation and have already spent the last 15 years in accelerating the money supply. However, the real inflation is evident from signs such as rising disparity between the rich and the poor and the shrinking of the middle class in the US. As the middle class is the hardest hit by inflation, so the results of inflation will be more evident in this group of people. To cheat the people, since the early 1990's, the government and Fed have been artificially reducing the outcome of the CPI (consumer price index). These steps include seasonal price adjustments, substitution of goods and so forth. The following graph shows today's CPI against its outcome based on its original calculation.

To deceive the American people, the policy makers have taken two more steps to alter the perception of real inflation. As the CPI is creeping up, they developed a "core CPI" index that essentially removes things that is an indication towards inflation, including essential items such as food and energy.

Now it is actually up to the Americans to decide how they would behave under the conditions. The US does not have free money and there will be a price to be paid for all the infusion of money in the economy and rising debts. Nor does the Americans we have a free banking system. As hyperinflation strikes, both the Federal Reserve and the government are going to probably destroy themselves in trying to prevent the inevitable.

However, the path to economic reconstruction will be an extremely difficult one especially for the middle class. The middle class should invest more in real money, ie in precious metals. As more and more individuals divert their money from government paper to something that is of actual value, the government and the Fed will be exposed for the fake institutions that they are. As a consequence, as the government fails, it will lead to an array of political problems. Unfortunately, the undereducated, misinformed, and the underprivileged will become the victims as they lack the resources to protect themselves. However, the middle class can save themselves by increasing their financial IQ and with a proper understanding of where to invest their money. Holding back dollars would be fatal as the dollar has started its inevitable slide downwards.

Contrary to what the policy-makers say, America is on an all-time low. American education is now falling with education itself becoming too costly to be afforded by the middle and the lower class of the society. Four decades ago the American family that thrived on a single high school graduate's income is long forgotten and in the middle class people are finding it difficult to maintain their standards of living if both the husband and the wife does not work. All these things, for which America was once revered, have been gradually eroded due to inflation.

OIL PRICES RISING OR DROPPING

History teaches us tough lessons as is evident from these facts. While the erstwhile Soviet Union emerged as the world's super power following the fall of Nazi Germany, the US (lone other superpower) suffered a major jolt when crude oil prices crosses $ 110 a barrel. Though the US remains the sole super power today, the fact remains that its abundant wealth was also due to factors like accessibility to cheaper oil and gas. History tells us that America was one of the leading producers of oil even generating so much so that it could export sizeable quantities to other countries. Crude oil was also the reason behind the rise of an MNC like Standard Oil Company of John D. Rockefeller (which was later reconstituted to emerge as Exxon Mobil). The same can be said about the powerful rise of the automobile, aviation industry together with agriculture.

But that oil which helped made America the super power and now the lone super power can be shaken by it. It would not take a war to shake America but oil. Oil production after hitting a peak in the 1970s has been on the downslide since then not recovering once except for some fall in oil prices externally by oil producing countries. On the other side is Russia which after fulfilling all its domestic needs has surplus crude to export to other countries which indicates the re-emergence of the former Soviet Union as a powerful nation. America has more worries on its hands as it must now also combat the growing prowess of Russia which is wielding the oil control. For a fact, Russia is consuming far less oil than it is producing. It has now become a power that is independent of its energy requirements. That perhaps explains the downgrading of ties by the George Bush administration with the Russia in 2001 including forcing nuclear and other weapons safeguards down the throats of the communists.   One must also remember that the American military powers are dependent on its fuel needs for its fighter planes, ground vehicles and hectors. The US Department of Defense is perhaps the single largest consumer of oil in the world. Right from the end of the Second World War, American claim to super power was fuelled by its huge energy reserves. Thus the costs of waging war on foreign soil was far cheaper back then than it is today which means the US government needs more money now to continue its war than it did ever before. The middle class bears the end of the brick stick. But now, all that Uncle Sam is doing is to pay unimaginable sums of money to foreign oil producers who are in turn investing in American assets! Assets that were built by America for its peoples. The Abu Dhabi Investment Authority made page one headlines in 2007 when it acquired a $ 7.5 billion stake in Citigroup, America's largest bank holding company. The Kuwait Investment Authority also acquired a multibillion-dollar stake in Citigroup, along with a $ 6.6 billion chunk of Merrill Lynch. According to U.S. Department of Energy data, the US is importing 12-14 million barrels of oil per day that is more than a billion dollars per day. This very fact makes it the biggest reason for the deficit and the fall of the US dollar. If oil prices rise any further our annual import bill could quickly approach three-quarters of a trillion dollars or more per year. While Americans spend about more than $ 3.23 per gallon of gasoline, Iraqis spend $1.36 per gallon for gasoline.

The worst part is that the U.S. military will need even more oil for the future wars it is planning to undertake. An American soldier in Iraq now uses about seven times as more oil per day than they did back in first Gulf War less than two decades ago. As the foreign military burden of the US keeps multiplying, so will the burden of deficit on the country. A point to note it that the era of cheap crude oil is over as is evident from the rising prices; from a modest $ 20 in 2002 to the "sky is the limit" benchmark. While the greens have always been giving dooms day predictions about depleting oil reserves in most of Organization of Petroleum Exporting Countries (OPEC) countries including Saudi Arabia, industry analysts have always spoken about rising prices. Today both of their predictions seem true as oil reserves are indeed depleting and it is now known that Saudi Arabia does not have enough oil reserves to meet the burgeoning crude oil demands globally. Analysts have always spoken about the limited oil supplies of the Saudis than was ever imagined by the US government. Books like 'Twilight in the Desert' spoke about these overwhelming dangers of dwindling oil reserves.

While Republicans and Democrats have always believed in just drilling the available oil reserves, it seems none of their Presidential candidates have had a clue about energy demands and supply. The simplest thing to do seems to wage a war against an oil rich country like Iraq. But such wars have only compounded the problems for the US even as its ramifications are being felt by the shrinking middle class. How else does one explain the profound distinction between election campaigns in the US? A case in point is the election campaigns of George Bush in the year 2000 when his comprehensive energy plan was virtually ceded by his Vice Presidential candidate, Dick Cheney clandestine Energy Task Force.

The drastically falling oil reserves and lack of foresight on part of politicians is giving rise to a neo liberal breed of independent analysts, industry big wigs, thinkers who pose faith in the doomsday predictions but are also concerned about the way the US government looks at and thinks about such issues. The unanimous thinking among such groups of people is that while oil reserves will not become zero any time soon but the times of getting oil barrels easily from OPEC countries is definitely over. That period is been left far behind. What is now needed is a paradigm shift in the ways one looks at these issues. A simple factoid is enough to bring about this shift in paradigm.

Consider this, as of today the straight deficit of the US Federal government is $ 4 trillion. The government is borrowing $ 3 billion everyday mainly to buy oil and gas. All this borrowing is going to be thrust on to the citizens of US who are already carrying enough burdens on their shoulders.

The ever rising prices of crude oil per barrel has risen from $ 20 in 2002 to a mind boggling $ 147 recently. Analysts now say that it is now no-holds barred affair as nobody can dare put a cap on the oil prices. Nobody can say at what point the rising prices will stabilize. It is the Vietnam War where no one could say when it is going to end. Or even like the quagmire in Afghanistan that the US finds itself today. There is a section of experts who are raiding their voices but the problem is that the US government does not want to hear them. May be they are not screaming enough or somebody is deaf. US policymakers will have none of it.

To add to the woes, an air of complacency descends on the lawmakers, every time there is a sharp fall in the oil prices. But alas the joy is short-lived as the fall just proves to be the lull before the storm. A strong wake-up call is perhaps the need of the hour which can pull everyone out of their deep slumber. Lest it becomes be too late to wake people up from this illusion. Even the media has this habit of speculating about the tumbling oil prices (on rare occasions when they are). That the Saudis are pushing their limits in meeting the oil demands of countries world wide needs to come to the fore. Their claims can no longer be taken for granted. If someone is smart enough in the Federal chain, all they would do was to sift through the fairy tales written by the Saudi geologists and how they create the mirage of endless oil reserves on their soil. Some guys did read these reports and made a million bucks writing books about them. Some estimates, mostly by the International Energy Agency (IEA) in Paris and the US government's very own Energy Information Association, say that the global oil demand would be pegged at more than 115 million barrels per day by the year 2030.

On a positive note, it is but apt that increasing demand will fuel rise in oil prices, the demand for oil has not hit the roof yet, if it may be termed so. Though there is no renewed spurt in demand from the home soil, nuclear powers India and China are filling the void with their ever escalating demand for oil. The IEA has pointed to this fact as it says that growing economies like India and China are not helping matters. And this demand from these nations is not likely to come down any time soon. Imagine a situation in the coming years where a deficit would arise in the demand and supply of oil! What will the US government then do? Boost its domestic production of oil? Well that is not a likely scenario as US hit its rock bottom in the 1970s itself when the demand and supply graph took a nose dive.

That such a scenario may arise soon is being dismissed by multi national companies who have taken recourse in a blitzkrieg of advertisements that seem to dismiss the prevalent notions. Whether they are doing this at their own peril only time will tell.

Nobody is disputing that oil production will start failing to meet the demand but when this would happen is for the lawmakers to give it a thought. If one talks about depletion rate on a average of oil producing fields, it is pegged somewhere between 4 % to 5 % per annum which means that new oil wells must be discovered to replace the depleting ones every day in the OPEC and other countries. There are many difficulties in assessing the depleting resources as one cannot rely on information provided by the stakeholders. Lack of transparency comes to the mind immediately.

What is in it for the middle income and low income groups in the US? The answer is simpler than it seems. To meet the shooting oil prices, the Federal government borrows more. The effect of which it prints more greenbacks to wipe the accumulating debts (already $ 4 trillion and counting) but this money does not reach the middle class. Inflation goes up but the middle classes do not have the monies to bear its brunt. Worse still, the Federal reserves cannot go for further cuts in the interest rates. There is a feeling that it has already pushed itself in a corner. A very tight corner. You push the consumers by higher oil prices and they respond by cutting back their spending. A situation which is not exactly viable for the present economy, one can safely conclude. Optimistic forecasts about increased consumer spending to boost the economy can be thrown out of the window.

A clear and present danger lurks which can only be quelled through delicate diplomacies of the government vis-à-vis the oil producing and controlling nations of the Arab world and beyond. Think about it, it is not just the economy but the inflating oil prices effects anything and everything including consumables to those goods that need to be transported. Peak oil prices also mean increase in air fare, gasoline not to mention and manufacture of fast moving consumer goods. Prices have more than quadrupled since 2002 and this seems to be heading only in vertical direction. Growth of businesses too gets in the line of fire as the fuel prices hit the bottom line too impacting potential to invest capital into businesses. Today, prices of many a raw material has increased in the US as fallout.

Of course the fact also remains that today the US is far more energy efficient by means of alternate fuels that it was five to six years ago. Bio-fuels also seem to be becoming cost effective at crude oil prices continue to surge ahead unabated. A weak dollar is contributing to the problems too as tensions in Iraq remain uncontained. War fears about American response to the rapidly changing political instability in Iran are worrisome. While impediments some are geopolitical in nature there are also geological worries like in Mexico for instance. Most of the OPEC members are hitherto doling out oil supplies to the maximum and there is no way this can be increased manifold. Saudi continues to be a mystery that does not have a happy ending.

What all this means is that be prepared to pay more for gasoline for your cars, pay a premium for your air tickets and couriers through FedEx. Prices of essential commodities like food are also known to rise steeply in accordance with the fuel prices as farmers have to spend more on gas. For a country like the US, consumer spending is the core of all economic activity. Given the higher oil prices, further recession also cannot be ruled out which is the last thing that working class need at this point of time. A strange paradox is being put in place whereby traditional oil producing countries like Saudi Arabia, Persian Gulf nations, Iran, Russia and even Venezuela are benefiting from the oil price rise, nations such as US are suffering due to it.

What all this also means is that the divide between the rich and every other class is mounting posing threats to the middle class: The Shrinking of the Middle Class. *The price of crude oil reached its highest level on an inflation adjusted basis in March 2008, when price per barrel touched $ 103.95. Average vehicle miles have risen steadily on a national basis since the 1970s while rates rose to more than 150 % between 1977 and 2001,* according to the Wall Street Journal. Thus the overriding effect of these surging oil prices impacts the US economy despite the fact that fuel efficiency levels are substantially increasing over the past few years. The world wide demand for crude oil is expected to top in the coming 3 to 20 years. There is also an assumption in certain quarters that some cities and regions would be better prepared than others in America. These are basically cities or regions that have better alternative fuel (and thus transport) modes. So, the realm of transportation is also under the cloud as an impact of the oil crisis (assuming that the further crisis is not brought about by US action on Iran). Commuting to office, college, super markets and malls is going to prove to be expensive soon enough. The time has come for Americans to increasingly look at alternate modes of transportation.

According to data complied by Associated Press, crude prices shot above $ 70 a barrel in the second week of September as a falling dollar pushed investors to commodities such as oil and gold. Benchmark crude for October delivery gained $ 3.27 to $ 71.29 a barrel on the New York

Mercantile Exchange. The dollar fell to a low for the year in the second against the Euro.

SOCIAL SECURITY AND MEDICARE GOING BANKRUPT

When President Franklin D. Roosevelt signed the original bill for social security in 1935 little must have he realized the impact it was going to have on the US economy. After more than seven decades, the picture is scary. Even by 2004, the US Social Security program had already paid out nearly $500 billion in benefits accrued under the program. It is not as if the problem has cropped up out of the blue, as social security (benefits for retirement, disability, death and survivorship) has been a major political issues during the reign of many a US Presidents including Gerald Ford, Jimmy Carter, Ronald Reagan, George H. W. Bush, Bill Clinton, George W. Bush and even the present incumbent Barack Obama.

The amount of dollars paid under the program is the most expensive one carried out by any government so far in the recorded history of mankind. Even now, social security program chunk is 37 % of the entire expenditure incurred by the Federal government. It can easily be likened to a mammoth exercise given its sheer size (it is estimated to keep 40 of aged America out of the tentacles of poverty). It also accounts for nearly 7 % of the Gross Domestic Product (GDP).

Despite reassurances, the matter of fact remains that Medicare is going bankrupt. According to industry watchers and analysts, it is expected to be $37 trillion in deficit by the year 2050 (it would be pertinent to note that the present total national debt is $ 9 trillion). The entitlements under the Social Security and Medicare programs are likely to bring about an explosion in the coming two decades. It is Medicare that is being seen to 'not sustainable' in the near future. The question everyone is asking is will the 80 million people born between 1946 and 1964 will bankrupt Social Security by the time, all the beneficiaries start receiving their benefits.

The first lot of the roughly 75 million baby boomers, a generation that has contributed fully to the Social Security and Medicare systems, has begun to retire while the money they contributed is actually gone!

By 2030, more than 80 million people would become eligible for social security which is an increase of 30 million people at this point of time. While a deficit of $ 4 trillion seems a difficult task today, imagine a burden of $ 50 trillion in the next 75 to 80 years.

Today, scores of baby boomers have been left shattered as their retirement plans have come to a naught. The fact is that many people have been left in a quandary and there is definitely no denying that. The ramifications are being felt in the housing market too. If people lose all their pension savings, significant adverse impact is bound to be seen on the housing market. We can soon expect to see glum looking city neighborhoods lying utter shambles as the elder lot may even be forced to come out of their retirement and start looking for part time jobs to ensure their sustenance. But poor economy coupled with current stock market scenario is making it extremely difficult for them to seek a re-entry into the job market albeit a part time job.

The math is quite simple actually. More than 79 million baby boomers have driven up housing demand. That trend is expected to reverse itself when these baby boomers are in the age bracket of 65 to 75 years. Also, there will be three sellers for each buyer in the coming times.

A study found that a quarter of people approaching retirement age are now expected to work until their 70s because their pension funds are shrinking. The global recession has also made its mark on the middle class as workers also have to put off their retirement plans to the economic meltdown world wide and escalating costs of living. Lawmakers, legal advisors these days cite how they are dealing with number of cases of the retirees losing their life savings to stocks or high risk linked investments products. Spending is now becoming laced with circumspection as baby boomers are not adding to their wealth while their asset values are nose diving by the day and their chances of redemption of a comfortable retirement life are receding everyday.

Irwin Goldsmith, 66, retired from the biotechnology industry expressed remorse that he had lost a lot in the stock market and also on his investments in some retirement funds. "I intend to cut down on spending on shopping, giving gifts to the kids and traveling around. Right now, there is not much I can do but just hope that the situation does not worsen any further," he lamented.

The stock markets which are spiraling downwards are not helping matters as Americans, mostly middle class, lost a few trillions. And this was major chunk of their retirement savings. The traditional pension plans, which have always been considered to be safer have been hit by the declining stock market, bringing to the fore another false notion. According to the Congressional Budget Office, pension plans have lost 15 % over the past one year due to tumbling markets. The burden on the middle class is higher in case of 401 (k) plans (defined contribution plans) due to the volatility of the stock markets. However, some analysts say that 401 (k) plans allow employees to take control of their retirements.

What this means is that the middle class will be forced to postpone their retirement plans and work for a longer period than they had imagined. Trillions of dollars of borrowed money is being spent by the country to shore up a battered economy. But as any good economist would know this spending of trillions of dollars will at best only continue to marginally spur the economy for a few more years. Even as dwindling of pension assets (a decline of 20 %) means more credit card debt, lack of accessibility to loans and declining value of realty.

As remarked by George Miller, chairman of the House Committee on Education and Labor, *"it is clear that Americans' retirement security may be one of the greatest casualties of this financial crisis."*

By the time President Barack Obama's term is over, the Social Security problem would already crippled the economy. A few years later, it would become a process that cannot be reversed. A continued fall in the footings of the fund is also likely to be an offshoot. Though the administration continues to treat these serious issues with kid gloves dismissing any talks of crises as unforeseen, many believe the process of negative impact on the economy has already begun. According to media reports, the Social Security's current annual surpluses of tax income over expenditures will begin to decline in 2011. This would then turn into rapidly growing deficits as the baby boom generation retires. It is also pertinent to note that the inadequate trust funds will steadily dwindle. The government bonds in these trust accounts will be presented to the Treasury for payment. But these payments can only be financed through bigger deficits, higher taxes or spending cuts. None of them is a good option.

The only policy of the present dispensation seems to wait till the time comes and till then talk about it. Presidents Bill Clinton and George Bush had spoken about it too and seems like Obama will keep talking about perils of diminishing Social Security if nothing but to keep the pot boiling. But the magnitude of the issue of Social Security continues to remain enormous as it the snowballing effect threatens to devastate the US economy.

This reminds of a certain Jamie Lawson – a worker investing in stocks who later started advising others from getting entrapped by brokers and investing in shares. Years later it now reminds of the 401 (k) enrollment plans of the administration. But the way the 401 (k) is set up, Lawson formula should apply to it as well. The Obama administration is hoping to get participation in individual retirement plans up to 80 % of Americans under the 401 (k) enrollment programs!

According to a study by AARP, which is a large interest and lobbying group, at least seven in 10 Americans older than 45 years expect they will have to continue to work beyond 65 years of age, the usual age of retirement. While mortality rates are on the upward trend in the US, people also have to work for longer number of years.

But then if several years ago much before the financial crisis happened, if someone had told you that the housing market was overvalued and derivatives were headed for cataclysm, would you have paid attention to it? It was not as if the best of the brains had not advised about this but nobody listened.

According to the Federal Reserve, *the assets held by the state and local governments' public pension plans declined by more than $ 300 billion between 2007 and 2008. Approximately 60 % of these funds are invested in stocks, 30 % in domestic fixed income securities and 5 % in real estate and the rest in other products.* It can be safely concluded that these findings have far fetched implications for the middle class families specially those workers who are nearing retirement. The Bureau of Labor Statistics says that *the people aged 55 and older who work full time rose significantly from 22 % in 1990 to about 30 % in 2007.*

The Employee Benefits Research Institute says that *in 2007, one in three American workers reported that they had not saved a single penny for their retirement.* Compare this to the year 2000 when 78 % of the workers had said that they had saved at least some money for their well being after retirement.

Another fact of the matter is that the Medicare is anything but unsustainable is amply proved by the fact that 45.7 millions Americans are currently without health insurance compared to 38.7 million in the year 2000 (sourced from US Census figures). The most worrying factor is that it is mostly the middle class that remain without either insurance or under insured. And this is mainly as people are increasingly finding healthcare way too expensive. On one hand, while healthcare premiums have increased manifold, wages particularly of the middle class have not been commensurate. The exponential rise in the cost of healthcare has also meant that employers are finding it difficult to provide medical cover for their employees. Now it is a known fact that healthcare costs are a major financial worry for the middle class so much so that they even lead to bankruptcy.

It is also a known fact world over that Americans have spend more than save less unlike countries like India where the governments worry about people just saving and not spending more. Americans have always had a history of low rate of personal savings which all the more explains the increased dependency on Social Security and Medicare programs of the US government.

The solution lies in understanding the dynamics of Medicare. From the government's perspective, the plan is to cut payments to hospitals. The administration hopes to save $110 billion in the coming decade. However, analysts differ on the cut in payments as they state that even as the revenues of hospitals is affected, there would not be much change as far as clinical care is concerned.

In fact, some would rather want the Social Security and Medicare to become bankrupt as the government is known to start thinking only when faced with a catastrophe. It is interesting to note that there are no provisions under existing laws to deal with financial imbalances as far as Medicare and Social Security are concerned.

The hope now is that markets not just in the US but world over will rise again from the economic slump and bring about much needed cheer to the people dependent on Social Security and Medicare programs.

Emanuel Collado

Savings being Wiped Out

As per the latest figures, the present recession has wiped out $2 trillion of retirement savings in the US and the US President has said that the Treasury Department would make it easier for workers to automatically enroll in an employee-sponsored 401(k) and other retirement plans, to use federal tax refunds to buy savings bonds directly, and to permit unused sick and vacation leave to be transferred directly to savings plans.

But how did US manage to land up in that situation on the first instant? The result was inevitable. With more and more money being pushed into the American economy, the situation has risen where the stock market has continuously tumbled to wipe out about $2 trillion in Americans' retirement savings in the past 15 months – a blow that means no early retirement for workers who will now have to stay on their job longer than planned, and check spending. The worst part is, for many middle class Americans, retirement savings is the only savings and they may well have to cut down drastically on their living expenses. The fall of the 401(k) asset, which declined by about 20 percent, is a major setback and it has taken the air out of most middle class citizens who are already reeling under the pressures of higher gas and food prices, increasing credit card debt, declining home values and less access to loans.

According to statistics, employees between the ages of 56 and 65 who had the fewest years on the job were the least affected as they had the least savings to show for, while those between 36 to 45 years, with the longest tenures, suffered the steepest declines.

Public pensions have not been left out of the loop. As per the Federal Reserve, the assets held by the state and local governments' pension plans have gone down by more than $300 billion between the second quarter of 2007 and the second quarter of 2008. About 60 percent of the public pension funds are invested in stocks, 30 percent in domestic fixed-income securities, 5 percent in real estate, and the remaining 5 percent in other products. The problem is most of the pension plans were to give the middle class a better retirement and the statistics look menacing for them.

According to many analysts, the most vulnerable workers are those nearing retirement, who have large balances in their retirement plans. These balances are now shrinking at a rapid rate. Due to inflation these middle class people are already running on tighter household budgets, which are also crippling them to a large extent.

According to a survey by AARP, 20 percent of baby boomers stopped contributing to their retirement plans in the past year because they have had trouble making ends meet. Already, more and more workers are delaying retirement. This is a trend that analysts and economists expect to go up by quite a few notches due to the problems that the US economy is facing. According to the Bureau of Labor Statistics the people age 55 and older who work full time grew from about 22 percent in 1990 to nearly 30 percent in 2007. By 2016, the bureau predicts, the number of workers age 65 and over will soar by more than 80 percent, and they will make up 6.1 percent of the labor force. In 2006, they accounted for 3.6 percent of active workers.

It should be noted that personal savings is also related to debts. According to statistics, the US household leverage, measured by the ratio of debt to the personal disposable income, had increased to a modest extent from 55% in 1960 to 65% in 1980s. However, over the next two decades, leverage more than doubled, reaching an all-time high of 133% in 2007. Such a rise in debt was coupled together by a steady decline in the personal saving rate. The combination of higher debt and lower saving enabled personal consumption expenditures to grow faster than disposable income, boosting up the economy. However, that boost, is clearly on a pile of debt. If Americans decide to consume more than they earn, they can do so only by borrowing money. That is what the US had done and people are now facing its consequences.

Over a period of time, consumption cannot grow faster than income because there is n limit to how much debt households generate, and that is based on their incomes. For a number of the US households, current debt levels appear too high. To achieve a sustainable level of debt relative to income, households may need to undergo a prolonged period of 'deleveraging', a process in which debts are reduced and savings are increased. But how is the middle class going to reduce debt when they are facing situations where maintaining their standard of living is becoming a problem in itself? Also, deleveraging comes with a price tag attached as it affects the growth rate of consumption.

The saving rate, now, should be able to push the debt-to-income ratio down to 100% over the next 10 years. Assuming an interest rate on the existing household debt of 7%, a future growth rate of the disposable income of 5%, and assuming that 80% of future saving is used for debt repayment, the household saving rate will have to rise from around 4% from the current situation to 10% by the end of the year 2018.

A rise in the saving rate of this level would eventually subtract about three-fourths of a percentage from the annual consumption growth each year: Taking the base year such in which the savings rate did not change. However, a larger subtraction from the consumption growth can be made to occur if we take the baseline with a declining savings rate.

In any case, these are mathematical probabilities. It would be very difficult in reality, to expect the people use 80% of their future savings on debt repayment. In a highly volatile market situation, in which the US economy is in now, coupled with the mortgage crisis and market crashes wiping away people's savings, the middle class is hard pressed even to maintain its standards of living, let alone increase their savings and pay debts.

However, the silver lining is US citizens may wake up to the fact that they will need to save. And as we will discuss further, their savings will have to be in precious metals such as gold and silver as the dollar has become too flimsy to be depended upon. Until recently, households in the

US were accumulating debt at too rapid a pace, allowing consumption to grow faster than income. An environment of easy credit, created by the Federal Reserve and the government facilitated this process. Consumption was also fueled by rising prices of stocks and housing, which provided collateral for even more borrowing. However, it should be noted that the value of the stocks and housing did not go up – only the money spent to buy them had gone up. Now both the government and the people are in the same soup. The value of that collateral, since not backed by something tangible, has since dropped dramatically, leaving many households in a precarious financial position, sweeping away their savings in chunks. The situation looks all the more menacing particularly in light of economic uncertainty that threatens their jobs. But the people might be waking to the fact of increasing savings and it seems probable that many US households, who can afford to, will reduce their debt and invest their money in precious metals. If accomplished through increased saving, the deleveraging process could result in a slowdown in consumer spending to a great extent.

THE HISTORY BEHIND IT ALL

In 1775, the American Revolutionary war began as America sought to gain independence. Out of the many reasons sited for the revolution, one particular cause stands out like a sore thumb among the rest. The then King George III of England outlawed he interest-free independent currencies that the colonies were running on; and, in turn, forcing them to borrow money from the Central Bank of England, with an interest attached. This immediately made 13 colonies of indebted to England. In the words of Benjamin Franklyn:

The refusal of King George III to allow the colonies to operate an honest money system, which freed the ordinary man from money manipulations, was probably the primary cause of the revolution.

Now, there is another institution that is manipulating the people of the US by manipulating money. It is the Federal Reserve or the Central Bank of the US. It is ironic to not that the Americans are doing the same thing for which they once fought against. So how did the Fed come into being? In secrecy, literally. In 1910 a secret meeting was held at the J.P.Morgan's estate on the Jekyll Island located off the coast of

Georgia. It was there that the central banking bill called the Federal Reserve Act was written in completely secrecy. This legislation was written by bankers and not law makers. This meeting was so secretive, so concealed from the government and public knowledge, that the 10-odd figures (it included the richest of the US) who attended disguised their names when in route to the island. After this bill was constructed, it was handed over to their political front man – Senator Nelson Aldrich – to push the bill through Congress. And in 1913, two days before Christmas when most of the Congressmen were at home enjoying with their families, the Federal Reserve Act was voted in and President Wilson, in turn, made it a law.

Later, President Wilson wrote:

[Our] Great Industrial nation is controlled by its system of credit. Our system of credit is privately concentrated. The growth of the nation, therefore, and all our activities are in the hands of a few men ... who necessarily, by very reason of their own limitations, chill and check and destroy genuine economic freedom.

Therefore, the Fed was established to make the rich richer. It was propaganda of the rich few, so they can amass wealth at the cost of ordinary citizens. When the government decides to bail out its rich friends such as the likes of Freddie, Fannie, AIG, et al, it turns to the Fed as that institution was set up by these rich people's forefathers for that particular reason – to help out rich friends.

Though America won its independence in 1793, its battle against the concept of Central Banks and the corrupt and greedy men and organizations associated with it have just begun. A central bank is the institution that produces the currency of an entire nation and therefore has the power to manipulate the economy for the gains of a few. Based on historical precedent, two specific powers are inherent in central banking practice:

- The control of interest rates
- The control of the money supply, or inflation.

The central bank does not simply supply a government's economy with money, it loans it to them at a rate of interest. Then through increasing and decreasing the supply of money, the central bank regulates the value of the currency being issued. It is critical to understand that the entire structure of this system can only produce one thing in the long run: DEBT. And as far as the US economy is concerned, the Federal Reserve had bee performing its duty with the greatest zeal.

However, it does not take advanced degrees in economics to figure their scam now. Every single dollar that is produced by the central bank is loaned out by the banks at an interest. That means every single dollar produced is actually the dollar plus a certain percent of debt based on that dollar, and this debt will increase will the passage of time. The central bank, however, has the monopoly of the production of the currency for the country and they loan out each dollar with an immediate debt attached to it. So where will the money that pay for that debt come from? It can, and has to come only from the central bank again. It means that the central bank has to perpetually increase its money supply to temporarily cover the outstanding debt created. This in turn, since that new money is loaned out at interest as well, creates even more debt? The end result of this system is slavery; for it is impossible for any government, and therefore the public, to ever come out of the self-generating debt.

According to Thomas Jefferson:

I believe that banking institution are more dangerous than standing armies... If the American people ever allow private banks to control the issue of currency... the banks and corporations that will grow up around them will deprive the people of their property until their children wake up homeless on the continent their fathers conquered.

By the start of the 20th century, the US had already experimented with the central banking System. The country had implemented and removed a few central banking systems, which were formed in the first place by ruthless bankers and the richest of the rich. At this time, among the richest among the rich in America were: Baron Rothschild, Paul Warburg, J.D. Rockefeller and J.P. Morgan – some of the richest families to come together ever in the history of the US with only one goal in mind. And in the early 1900's they decided to push the legislation once again to create another central bank. However, they knew the government and public had already seen the intrinsic deformities of such a system. Thus they decided to manufacture problems in the economy to influence public opinion. J.P.Morgan, who was considered a financial luminary at that time, exploited his mass influence by publishing rumors that a prominent bank in New York wasn't solvent or bankrupt. Morgan new this would cause mass hysteria which in turn will effect other banks I the process. And unfortunately, he was right. The public, afraid to lose their deposits and life savings, immediately began mass withdrawals. Consequently, the banks were forced to call in their loans thus started the spiral of bankruptcies, repossessions and turmoil emerged – only because a few rich men, who were already the richest, wanted to become richer.

The panic of 1907 led to the Congressional investigation headed by Senator Nelson Aldrich. Not surprising, tjis particular Senator was as corrupt as his rich friends and had intimate ties to the banking cartels and later became part of the Rockefeller family through marriage. The commission in its report recommended a central bank should be implemented so that a panic like 1907 could never happen again. This was the spark that international bankers needed to initiate their plan. As mentioned earlier, after the secret meeting, in 1913, with heavy political sponsorship by the bankers, Woodrow Wilson became President, having already agreed to sign the Federal Reserve Act in exchange for campaign support. So now we see that the US economy and the present crisis are based on lies and cheating and fooling the people in every crooked possible ways for – Money.

After having the system set in place, the rich people went about their job to become richer. As always, the American people were told lies. The public was told that the Federal Reserve System was an economic stabilizer while inflation and economic crises were a thing of the past. Well, life comes in a full circle and as history has shown, nothing was further from the truth. The fact is, the international bankers used the Fed as a streamline machine to expand their personal ambitions. For example, from 1914 to 1919 the Fed increased the money supply in the economy by nearly 100% resulting in extensive loans to small banks and the public and setting into motion the inevitable result of accumulation of debt. Then, in 1920, the Fed called in huge amounts of the outstanding money from the economy resulting in the supporting banks calling huge loans and just like 1907, collapse occurred. This was done on desire and the design of the people who had put the system in place. Banks outside of the Federal Reserve System collapsed consolidating the monopoly of the small group of international bankers.

However, as history reveals, the panic of 1920 was just a warm-up. From 1921 to 1929 the Fed again increased the money supply resulting once again in extensive loans to the public and banks and setting in motion the process of money creation. They also introduced the margin loan in the stock market. This type of loan allowed an investor to put down only 10% of the stock's price, while the remaining 90% being loaned from the broker. In other words, a person could own a $1000 worth of stock, with only $100 as payment. This method became popular in the 1920's as everyone seemed to be making money. However, the catch to this loan was that it could be called in at any point of time and would have to be paid within 24 hours. Termed as 'a margin call' the result was the selling of the stock purchased with the loan. So, a few months before October 1929, J.D.Rockefeller, Bernard Baruch and other insiders exited the market. And on October 24th, 1929 the New York financiers who furnished the margin loans started calling them in, en mass. This sparked an instantaneous massive sell off in the market and markets crashed. It also triggered mass bank runs collapsing over 16.000 banks enabling the rich conspirators to not only buy up rival banks at the discount but to also buy up whole corporations at pennies on the dollar. It was the greatest robbery ever committed in the history of American. But that didn't stop there. Rather then expanding the money supply the Fed contracted it, fuelling the great depression.

Having reduced the society, the Federal Reserve bankers decided that the gold standard should be removed to give them all the freedom they would need to manipulate the society and economy. Therefore, under the pretense of helping to end the depression, came the 1933 gold seizure whereby in one sweep, the Federal Reserve captured all the gold. Under the threat of imprisonment the Americans were forced to turn in all gold bullion to the Treasury. The Fed robbed the public of what little wealth they had left. And at the end of 1933 the gold standard was abolished. That made the dollar legal tender which means it is backed by nothing – a worthless piece of paper with fancy diagrams on them. Since the only thing that gives a currency its value is how much of it is in circulation, the power to regulate money supply is also the power to regulate its value which is in turn the power to bring entire economies and societies to its knees just by releasing or calling back those pieces of paper on which only the Fed has the authority.

The Fed is, it will be important to note, a private organisation and not under the control of the government. It is a private bank that loans all the currency at interest to the government, without any sense of ethics, and is completely consistent with the fraudulent central banking model that the country sought to escape from when it declared independence. Now the Federal Reserve Act was not the only unconstitutional bill pushed through Congress, they also pushed the Federal Income Tax, which is completely unconstitutional as it is a direct unapportioned tax.

All direct taxes have to be apportioned to be legal. Secondly, the required number of states in order to ratify the amendment to allow the Income Tax was never met. At present, day roughly 35% of the average worker's income is taken from them via this tax. In other words a worker works 4 months out of the 12 to fulfill this obligation. And the money goes to pay the interest on the currency being produced by the fraudulent Fed, a system that was created just to protect the Fed so that the plundering by the rich could go on unabashed. The money that the Americans pay working 4 months a year goes literally into the pockets of the international bankers who own the Fed. Interestingly, there is no law in existence that requires you to pay this tax. This also tells us how ignorant the general American is about their economy and the judiciary system.

MORTGAGE CRISIS AND THE MIDDLE CLASS FAMILY

President Barack Obama speaking about the home mortgage crisis in Phoenix, Arizona in February 2009 pointed out saying *"the American dream is being tested by the mortgage crisis that not only threatens the stability of our economy but also the stability of families and neighborhoods. It is a crisis that strikes at the heart of the middle class; the homes in which we invest our savings, build our lives, raise our families and plant roots in our communities."* The home mortgage was the last thing the middle class in the current economic scenario.

Consider this J. T. Walsh, 71, and his wife Sara Walsh, 62, a retired couple, were living with their two grandchildren in their Indiana for more than a decade. Two years ago, they received a call from a mortgage consulting company that offered to re-finance their home loan through the mortgage route. The monthly mortgage quoted by the company was six times less the monthly loan payment the Walsh family was incurring.

But to get the lower rate for monthly payment, they were asked to shell out a lump sum amount initially for the first two months which the couple paid by borrowing on their credit cards. After receiving the payments for two months, the mortgage company refused to refinance their home loan into a lower monthly mortgage. Soon enough, their home was snatched from the elderly couple after they were evicted by the mortgage company and they were forced to seek refuge by paying nearly $ 1,000 per month as rent.

Heart rending stories like these are becoming quite a common feature across the US these days. *"So many Americans have shared with me their personal experiences of this crisis. Many have written letters or emails or shared their stories with me at rallies and along rope lines. Their hardships and heartbreaks are a reminder that while this crisis is vast, it begins just one house – and one family – at a time. It begins with a young family – maybe in Mesa, or Glendale, or Tempe – or just as likely in suburban Las Vegas, Cleveland, or Miami. They save up. They search. They choose a home that feels like the perfect place to start a life. They secure a fixed-rate mortgage at a reasonable rate, make a down payment, and make their mortgage payments each month. They are as responsible as anyone could ask them to be,"* President Obama had remarked in that speech in Arizona. The stories continue to happen.

According to some estimates, the American sub-prime mortgage crisis would ultimately lead to an estimated 2.2 million people losing their homes to foreclosures in the next couple of years like it was the case with the Walsh family. More than a million homes had some kind of foreclosure action taken against them in the year 2007. Two years later, this number is only swelling.

Like President Obama said in that Arizona speech of his, it is becoming an increasingly difficult situation as neither are the affected people able to leave their homes nor are they able to stay on. Timely payment means that savings get thrown out of the window. And when credit cards are also used up, the only option left is to default on payments.

The phenomenon of sub-prime mortgages has evolved and snowballed into a major issue within a sport span of time. The process perhaps began in the early 1990s and then expanded greatly during the past few years. Sub-prime mortgage loans, as is common knowledge, have far higher interest loans. They also have higher fees and penalties than the conventional mortgages. As there are scores of middle class people who do not qualify for traditional mortgages (due to their income or credit history), sub-prime mortgage is the only way out for them. Worse still, these sub-prime mortgages are being sold as an American Dream for many years now. But the higher interest rates and other costs have driven many families who took sub-prime mortgages into situations where they were forced to give up their houses.

More than one-fifth of all mortgages in the U.S. were already sub-prime by 2006. It is mostly first time house buyers who fall for the sub-prime mortgage loans and those middle class seeking re-finance of their existing conventional mortgage loan.

The sub-prime mortgage crisis has spread its tentacles to the stock market and industry as well as they is linked to the house marketing. A robust economy needs the housing industry to thrive. All this in turn affects the spending or purchasing of the masses which again bodes ill for the tumbling economy.

President Obama in his crisis plan for rescuing American families has announced that the administration would only help those *"who have played by the rules and acted responsibly; by refinancing loans for millions of families in traditional mortgages who are underwater or close to it; by modifying loans for families stuck in sub-prime mortgages they can't afford as a result of skyrocketing interest rates or personal misfortune; and by taking broader steps to keep mortgage rates low so that families can secure loans with affordable monthly payments,"* to put in Obama's own words.

The foreclosure situation in the present sub-prime mortgage crisis is now being viewed not just as a long known practice of economic and housing discrimination, but as discrimination by banks and other institutions to snatch away properties from communities and peoples who are an oppressed lot.

For many years now, the financial institutions of American capitalism brought in red tape into the system thus denying mortgages, business loans, and other services to people living in poor or middle class neighborhoods. Many feel that it was a deliberate scheme of the profit-driven workings of capitalism that have devastated the inner-city communities of oppressed people.

The current crisis also brings to the fore an interesting aspect of the economic divide that still exists between whites and Black people in America. When one considers that homeownership and home equity is the primary, even sole, asset of many Black and Latino families, this focuses up even more sharply the devastating effect of the sub-prime crisis on Black and Latino communities. However, it may be noted that it is not just low-income Blacks and Latinos who have been victimized.

Then there is also another side of the same coin worth taking a look at. A consumer gets a mortgage loan, the mortgage company or the bank sells the loan to an investment bank where it is clubbed with a pool of similar other loans. The investment bank then sells its bonds in the market that are backed by the payment on those mortgages. In America, securities piggy backing on assets currently account for a third of entire fixed-income market, according to some analysts.

The sale of such mortgage loans to investment banks curtails the mortgage companies' risk of holding bad debts offered by it to less qualified home buyers. Herein lies the crux of the problem as it is known to encourage unacceptable business practices by banks and mortgage companies while artificially increasing demand for housing. The decline of the housing market subsequently has focused on the tightening the noose of credit and the resulting decrease of realty values. This very thought that the US bond market is exposed to the credit volatility of borrowers was mostly going unnoticed until recent market crash.

While the focus so far has been on the sub-prime mortgages as if to suggest that middle class of American perhaps bears entire responsibility for so all the market volatility. It is interesting to note that more than 4 % of all mortgage loans slightly above sub-prime are also in doldrums.

On the other hand, the foreclosures situation is also bound to impact roughly more than two million school going children as mortgage foreclosures and evictions by mortgage companies would result in the parents of the kids moving away to other cities, places or regions. Under federal law, school districts are required to have homeless education liaisons to identify and assist homeless students. There has been a steady increase in the number of homeless students who are seeking State assistance for continuation for their studies which also a major worry especially for the middle class. As per the data available with the National Association for the Education of Homeless Children and Youth, a grassroots membership and advocacy organization, conducted its survey of more than 1,000 school districts about the impact of the foreclosure crisis. These districts reported serving a total of about 250,000 homeless students as of April 2008.

"At least 300 districts that responded to the survey said that the foreclosure crisis was having 'some or significant impact on homelessness. Others weren't sure why the numbers were going up, whether it was due to foreclosures or the economy, or both," as per this data. Prominent fallout of the home mortgage crisis due to the constant moves from one city to another by parents of kids who lost out their homes to foreclosures has been the behavioural in nature and also impacting learning capabilities. The Government Accountability Office finds similar negative impacts on math performance of school kids. The biggest worry though is the likely housing instability that may have large spread ramifications for a nation struggling to improve its 70-percent average high school graduation rate, which dips to 50 percent in many of the largest U.S. cities. Better housing facilities are also known to wean away kids from violent ways and crimes, according to some analysts.

It is but obvious that once a person loses his housing and alternate means of accommodation are not exactly forthcoming, savings are broken and often families may get split up among several relatives and friends. That is when *they learn that acting responsibly often isn't enough to escape this crisis. Perhaps someone loses a job in the latest round of layoffs, one of more than three and a half million jobs lost since this recession began or maybe a child gets sick, or a spouse has his or her hours cut. In the past, if you found yourself in a situation like this, you could have sold your home and bought a smaller one with more affordable payments. Or you could have refinanced your home at a lower rate. But today, home values have fallen so sharply that even if you made a large down payment, the current value of your mortgage may still be higher than the current value of your house. So no bank will return your calls, and no sale will return your investment,* according to President Barack Obama.

Virginia Randolph, a divorced mother of two in Detroit, Michigan has for the last few years run her day care business from her home. In 2006, as her business multiplied, she bought a $ 500,000 four-bedroom house solely because her credit score of 600 provided her an adjustable-rate mortgage from a mortgage company even though she had no money for a down payment. But as the region's economy slowed down, Randolph's business slowed with it. She fell behind on her mortgage payments and eventually faced foreclosure from the mortgage company. Randolph's housing woes are only adding to her recent divorce. She is now closing working with a housing advocacy organization in a bid to re-negotiate a mortgage modification. In case that does not happen, she has applied for public housing.

She says the worst part about leaving is that her children would no longer be in this school district, which was the main reason she moved to the vicinity. As per existing federal laws, her children would not have to change schools. Currently a debate is raging in the Senate regarding brining about an amendment to the McKinney-Vento legislation that would add $ 30 million in funds to school districts to cater to the homeless students and meet their transportation needs.

The sub-prime and foreclosures situation is a tangible result of the downward slide of home values, the fact that banks and mortgage companies were taking everyone for a ride has also come to the fore. Amidst this ever deepening crisis, the need of the hour is accountability on part of mortgage companies and banks, responsibility on part of the borrowers and regulation by the government.

As the US economy crashes, all debates have been put off regarding whether the recession is going to be mild or deeper. It is pretty evident from the information as discussed above that this is going to be much longer, uglier and deeper and lasting at least four quarters and more. The whole economy has been inflated to an enormous extent and the Americans are not likely to resolve the situation soon. With various problems existing in the economy and each of these problems depends on the other, the situation is pretty complex. More so for the middle class and the lower middle class for they, as usual, are going to be the worst hit among the lot. Shrinking of the middle class is just a small signal of this economy and is more an indicator that the economy has become grossly unbalanced due to faulty economic policies favoring only the rich. The recession will definitely be protracted and painful as a debt-burdened, shopped-out and less-saving consumer is on the ropes; while the financial system is on the verge of a crisis which is going to cause a severe credit crunch. Massive losses to the money market funds and other financial institutions will be the feature; and corporate defaults and junk bonds will trigger massive losses on credit default. The eventual losses in the US financial system may add up to more than $1 trillion. The rest of the world will also not be spared, and the real and financial contagion from the US to the rest of the world will be serious. Economies such as India and China had been gaining from jobs exported out of US. As the economy of US collapses, there will be shockwaves and repercussions worldwide. The Fed may try its best to undo the monster it has created. However, movements in the monetary policy are not likely to deal with the deep credit and insolvency issues that plague the US economy. The US and global equity markets are bound to enter a serious bearish market as a US recession and global economic slowdown take a toll on investors and firms.

A Doomed Program Called Mortgage

Following months of blind alleys, dejection and running away from representatives of his bank, Sam Miller is still trying to re-work his loan. When Sam lost his job as a social scientist, he and his wife left their northern California home in August 2008 and relocated to New Jersey where he found a new job. And since then, he has never again missed repayment on the two-bedroom home in California though its value has come down by about 50 %. But his wife lost her job due to the move; he decided to call his bank to find out if the bank could re-adjust the loan to lower the monthly installments which they promptly refused. So, Sam approached several other bank representatives on a regular basis. But he says he always got confusing responses from them. A bank loan he was supposed to get in a few days did not materialize. At one point, after assurances that he submitted all the appropriate paperwork, he was told a form was missing.

When he provided the missing paper, he was told the remaining paperwork was more than 30 days old and he would have to update and resubmit each form. At another point, he was told his file showed a bad credit card debt that he actually did not owe! After his latest rejection he asked for an explanation from the bank officials who told him that the investors holding his mortgage were of the opinion that he spent too much on clothing. This is story of many middle and upper middle class families in the US. Despite what the government claims are its best efforts, the problem of foreclosures and mortgage crisis is definitely not over. And it is turning out to be a major disappointment for millions of Americans. And these millions stand to lose their homes in the coming months. The lending banks and mortgage companies just want to impose the foreclosure clauses and evict the borrowers. They just refuse to re-adjust or bring in modifications in the loans granted to the middle and upper middle class families.

There are government guidelines to the lending banks and mortgage companies to comply with so as to ensure justice to the borrowers. Banks and mortgage companies generally get away citing that there has been some miscommunication or confusion on part of the customer and everything will soon be set right. After a few months, they impose foreclosure and take away people's homes from them just like that.

This frustration is also shared by professionals who are trying to help the borrowers re-adjust their loans and mortgages. Though the housing market is going crumbling, the pace of foreclosures is not relenting. As per some estimates, more than 13 % of property owners with a mortgage are either behind schedule on their payments or in stage of foreclosure. And this figure is spiraling every month with more and more people defaulting on their mortgages. The continuing rise in foreclosures delays any meaningful recovery in the American economy. This is housing is one of major reasons for a downturn if things are in a bad shape.

Every new foreclosed home adds up as unsold asset in the market and eats into demand for newer properties. Likewise, foreclosed homes sold at ridiculously low prices or in distress sales bring down the market rates for houses. This is will not stop till the rate at which foreclosures are taking place is arrested or stunted. Till then middle class America will keep in mortgage many times more than the current worth of their asset. According to data in a recent research report by Deutsche Bank about half of all house owners in the country will face foreclosures by the year 2011. Sliding prices of houses will also mean that all the current owners of properties will lose out in the battle against home equity. House owners then are forced to take tough decisions like selling off their houses while they can still get some respectable prices. There will be a horde of people trying to sell off their second properties or even the first ones just to make through the recession. But selling properties at a loss means that these people will be unable to relocate for a new job, buy a bigger house for an expanding family or downsize for a planned retirement because they cannot afford to sell their home for a loss.

When John Hyde's son, Henry died last year, he faced a difficult battle selling his son's Georgia, Atlanta home, which was bought for

$150,000 in the year 2000. This year, Hyde got an offer that was $10,000 less than the original price of the property. But with so many foreclosed properties in the neighborhood, the appraisal came back at just $75,000, and the deal fell through. *"There was a house very close from my son's place and was like a three bedroom house but it sold for $26, 000,"* he said.

Hyde said he was unable to work out a loan adjustment with the lending bank and ultimately the he was forced to sell off for $100, 000 at a foreclosure auction which still left him with some equity to settle his son's estate.

"I had no choice," he lamented. *"I had to sell the house. There were bills to pay with the money gotten from the sale,"* he said.

The disappointment with mortgage relief plans of the government has also forced desperate house owners to sell off their homes in foreclosure auctions which are proving to be quite a scam. Incidents related to mortgage fraud have hit an all time high as well. The Making Home Affordable (MHA) program is supposed to offer troubled borrowers two possible solutions. The Home Affordable Modification Program (HAMP) is designed to lower payments on existing loans by cutting the interest rate and stretching out the term. The Home Affordable Refinance Program (HARP) gives borrowers who are current on their payments but stand to default in the coming months to restructure their loan with some adjustments. The program pays enticements of several thousand dollars for each adjusted loan to mortgage servicers, which are on several occasions not the same lenders who hold the mortgage.

The downside of the program is that while Obama administration unveiled it recently, neither was much time given to train servicers nor was any advance notice given to them about the implementation plan of the government. Worst of all, key components of the program were still not in place when the program was unveiled while some of the initial guidelines limited the program and its potential to help people affected by the foreclosures crisis. Another problem was that too many cases flooded the servicers who did not have the wherewithal to handle the emerging situation. The number of requests landing on the tables of these servicers is astounding, incredible even. But all these requests need to be attended to else what purpose would have the program served people with grievances have nowhere to go. Then there is also the issue who those who unnecessarily flood applications under the program but change their plans when they are contacted by the servicers.

Staffing is also a major issue at the Treasury's Homeownership Preservation Office, which was set up to look into the quick rise in foreclosures in the country. The Making Home Affordable program was proposed by the Barack Obama government and enacted by the Congress after two earlier administration-sponsored efforts in the Hope Now Alliance and the Hope for Homeowners program which failed to substantially bring down the high rates of foreclosure rate. Hope Now which was unveiled in October of 2007 has amended several hundred thousand mortgages, although the so-called re-default rate from the first round of modifications were as high as 50 %.

The Hope for Homeowners program, commenced in July 2008, was expected to reach 400,000 suffering mortgage holders. In the initial stages, the program was hindered by burdensome terms and red-tapism. Only one homeowner found help from this program! The stipulations were relaxed later but they served no meaningful purpose. Later the Federal government announced that it was re-writing the program yet again! The unchecked rise in foreclosures also is destroying the value of assets backed by mortgages that are held by banks and private investors.

Till now, bulk of the investors has been refusing to take absorb the losses on the face and bring down the quantum of loan for property owners who owe far more in mortgage than their house is worth in the current market. Despite the fact that most of the major lenders and servicers have signed and ratified the MHA program, the move to make a loan or mortgage more affordable or forgive some of the principal amount is entirely voluntary. So it is up to these lenders and mortgage investors and mortgage company owners to pull people out of their misery. While investors may claim that they have suffered losses due to their investments on mortgages, these losses are only on paper, according to some analysts. These investors are just waiting for these losses to begin to dissolve even as the housing market recovers. But what such a thing is instead doing is to continue to aggravate the foreclosure troubles and further hurt an economy that is already witnessing a major downturn.

That unfathomable recession has intensified the rate of foreclosures in America. When the mortgage market began melting down in the later part of 2006, many of those in default were sub-prime mortgage borrowers and those who were sold adjustable loans that allegedly were reset to unaffordable payments. With over seven million jobs obliterated by sub-prime mortgage, housing crisis and tumbling of the housing market, people losing their paychecks have become a thorn in the flesh for those groups that are trying to bring down and curtail the rate of foreclosures across America. The National Foundation for Credit Counseling now says that the MHA program still needs some fine tuning to be done to serve its purpose in the truest sense of the term especially for those employees (mostly middle class) who have experienced a severe reduction of their incomes. This has thus brought about skepticism among the house owners who seriously doubt the help that would be ultimately trickle down to them.

According to the own estimates of the White House as many as 40 % of the more than 10 million house owners who are likely at risk of default and foreclosure could be helped. What was the basis of their estimation is questionable given the present scheme of things. But some other estimates indicate that only 20 % of the loans serviced for modification or re-finance were genuine applicants with no malice. Under the existing guidelines and norms, borrowers must compulsorily prove that they can devote a mandatory 31 % of their income to their newly devised monthly mortgage re-payment plan. Some experts say that this benchmark is way too high and suggest that the Treasury should bring down the cap to 25 % to qualify more homeowners. For whatever reason, voluntary efforts to modify loans have proceeded at a snail's pace.

Very few mortgage borrowers say that they had seen their mortgages modified as per the new program designed for this very purpose. This is also reflected in the data released by the Treasury. For instance, a giant bank which is one of the largest holders of house mortgages could modify about only 4 % of eligible borrowers as of last month. There were also some lenders who had not modified a single loan. All this goes to prove that there is an urgent need for stricter measures and an eagle eye regulation and monitoring of all the stakeholders involved in this very critical process.

The point is that the systems for ensuring accountability are non-existent and that in itself is a fundamental flaw of the plan. A plan that is voluntary in nature, lack of controlling factors and authorities overseeing the program, and no comprehensive processes established to re-assure the borrowers looking to seek remedy from the program. The carrot approach of the administration to curtail foreclosures by offering $50 billion in incentives to servicers for modifying loans was only adopted after the financial services industry successfully fought back a powerful stick that would have granted bankruptcy judges authority to modify the terms of a mortgage loan from the bench. One should note that judges can pass judgments in any other form of consumer debt in a bankruptcy proceeding but not mortgages.

THE NEW WORKING POOR

Torea Frey was a New Yorker and a shopaholic. Coming from a middle class background, a decade back she had no problems in spending and earning and keeping it going that way. "I used to reach the maximum limit on my three credit cards at the end of every month. I have been trying to clear off my debts, but somehow, I have not been able to," she confesses. However, credit cards had never been a major problem to her as she could clear off some at the beginning of every month when she got her pay working as a fitness trainer. On the other cards she used to just pay the minimum and get along.

But that was the time when the economy was booming. Now it is recession.

And in 2009, she is a single mother, getting half of what she used to get a few years back and has to take up a part-time job of working n a local grocery in the evenings and weekends.

"The recession has hit hard and people tell me that I have become a working poor," she says. She had to take up the part-time ob just to pay her debts and feed her family without any savings. If the recession is so hard now, what will happen if it deepens – she wonders. The answer is anybody's guess – it will become harder.

According to the estimates of the government, about 37.3 million people in the US were living in poverty in 2007. This comes to about 12.5 percent of the population. The US government defines poverty as an annual income of $21,203 or less for a four-member family. Analysts estimates that the percentage will rise by at least half a percentage as compared to that of last year. And the number is only going to go up as more and more people slip into poverty from the middle class – just like Ms Frey. So much so, that the society has already coined a name for these people – the working poor.

Ms Frey is a typical example of what is happening and is going to happen with many of the middle class families in the coming years as the recession takes a grip on the economy. "Many of the decisions that seemed so right at that point of time seems horribly wrong now. No body was concerned with the debts that I was in and the air was everybody is indulging, so why shouldn't I? She makes monthly installment payment on her car, whose value is now less than the amount she owes on it. O top it all, "I have slashed my retirement contributions to $6 per check from $90," she says, partly in due to the drop in the stock market and partly to feed her family. However, the conditions that the US is facing now, her savings might not have saved or prepared her for the future, though, that is the only savings that she had accumulated over the years.

The numbers of these working poor are swelling as more families slip into poverty. Health benefits are lost and employees with wages on the lower side bear the brunt of many corporate cutbacks. Many of these had been families dwelling in the middle class. But due to the recession have faced job cuts and have slipped into poverty. This whole situation means more employees, with many of them in service jobs that are essential to the economy, are working full-time, but still cannot support their families.

The fate of these so called working poor is becoming a major issue for politicians, union groups and activists – as they are not going to diminish in the near future, but are going to go up. There have been public outcry to some extent and lobby groups have been calling for reforms. Unions are taking an effort to preserve the benefits and boost pay for service-sector jobs. The rise in low-wage workers has also acted as a catalyst to push people down the ladder. Activists who are waging campaigns to pass living-wage ordinances –local laws that require some of the firms and the businesses to pay their employees more than the minimum wage of $5.15 an hour.

It is fascinating that the change in the economy has created a new breed of the poor. This is a class, who, unlike the real poor, wants to work and is working, but is being deprived of leading the same livelihood that they were having a decade back.

Wages have also eroded constantly and have not increased, though productivity has risen. According to statistics, the value of the minimum wage peaked in the late 1960s, which means that workers today, who earn minimum wage, have a less buying power than in the years before. And the fall of the dollar had a lot to do with this situation too. After adjusting for inflation, the value of the minimum wage rate an hour – $5.15 – is 24% lower today than it was in 1979. Therefore, a full-time worker earning at the minimum wage rate will earn $10,712 a year, which is below the 2002 federal poverty line of $11,756 for a family of two.

On the other hand, welfare rolls have dropped by more than 50% since 1994, pushing many of the former recipients of the rolls into jobs that pay low wages. These are employees who work as security guards, hotel workers, receptionists, food processors, data-entry clerks and all.

Among other challenges, low-wage workers cannot avail most of the benefits that are available to higher earners. For example, more than half of poor workers, working welfare recipients and workers who recently left welfare are not eligible to take paid leave from their jobs. While lower interest rates have made homeownership more affordable for many belonging to the higher middle class, runaway prices have put homes out of reach for the working poor. According to statistics, in the past 12 years home prices have risen 30% faster than wages and salaries for middle income and lower middle income families.

RECESSION AND THE MIDDLE CLASS

What has the recession meant for the middle class in America, well it just made many of them broke. News about recession is floating in the air; it is in the newspapers, on television channels and most importantly in our daily lives. Banks are downing shutters, financial institutions are going under the hammer prior to filing of bankruptcy and businesses are shrinking in size and volumes. There have been immense layoffs in an endeavor to save money or people are turning up for work only to be given pink slips or circulars that their company will close before the end of the month.

It takes two paychecks to make ends meet in our contemporary society and if a person in the family loses a job it will affect everyone at home. In many places, employees are shell shocked up on finding their company locked up with a sign directing them where they collect their final pay. In case, one is not able to pay his home mortgage, foreclosure clauses will ensure that the property will be lost to the lender and his family left homeless. If the car payment is missed for the third time it is repossessed and one is left to fend for himself without any transportation mode available to reach workplace.   Children become the victims of psychological pressures as their parents scramble to find some a roof over their head, but having exhausted their credit limit on their credit cards, renting a cheap hotel room is a distant dream.Where does it stop? How will the middle class weather this recession? Perhaps only time will tell. If someone lives to tell the tale, conceivably he or she made the early moves. If one does not want to lose his home then he better make it priority no matter what. It is definitely going to be hard with some tough decisions that needed to be taken. First on the list is to take cognizance of one's income.

Compute the quantum of cash coming into the household that goes into paying the mortgage payment. Other expenses that require cash are electricity, gas. Food is essential and attire is of minor significance as most people have more than enough. Then again hopefully, pink slips stay out of the way. Most of us live paycheck to paycheck already so start a jar, box, bank, drawer or something that you can stick $ 10 in each paycheck. It may not seem like much at the initial stages, but when one is broke these little side savings would come in handy. This is the basic emergency money for small items like gas in the car, one small bill paid or for medicines.

One can always try to pick a second job a few hours a night or on a day off. This is not for extra money to spend but for security. The second job is also for exigencies and for times when your normal job cuts to part time. With two part time jobs any one can make ends meet a lot better. Now, it is a well accepted notion that one should have at least three months living expenses in a savings account. Hobbies are another great way to earn some extra income. Jobs like repairing cars, making wedding cakes is always welcome. The trick is not to charge much or it may affect the business. Charges need to be reasonable while still ensuring a profit.   If one is thinking about changing careers then it is to be made sure that there is a need for such a service. The medical field is good option to pursue but caution is to be exercised if one is looking at the billing field as most of it is now outsourced to countries like India. Truck driving and management are a few of the better alternatives in the job market in these times of recession.

Entrepreneurship is always welcome particularly so for the women folks. One should look into business grants that need to be re-paid, low interest loans among other things. Choosing a business that can be run from the home is an easy way out ensuring minimal overheads. Renting or leasing should not exaggerate the space needed to set shop. Making a business affordable and then making it work is the mantra. There are several business models that can work within a small area All said and done, there is no denying that entrepreneurship is a superlative way to beat recession blues.

Service sector services like yard care, cleaning, sewing, cooking, companion care, babysitting, childcare, shopping service, bookkeeping, phone work, car repair, piano tuning, music lessons or just about anything for the community. Each of one of these jobs will bring in enough extra money to pay bills and buy food for home.

If the value of a new car coupled with payments is higher than most mortgages then it makes sense to sell off the car.

It is not just about Economics

The shrinking of the middle class is not just about economics alone. It is also about a lot of factors involved. As explained in previous chapters, the present status of the US economy displays one of the largest income inequalities in the history of the country. The gap between the rich and the poor is almost as much as was recorded in the 1920s, also known as the roaring 20s.

That decade was undoubtedly so, with naked display of wealth owned by a few businessmen at the expense of the common people. People such as Rockefeller, Morgan and Carnegie had amassed huge wealth by manipulation the laissez faire economy. With no government regulation, these capitalists stole from the common people cleverly and quickly due to the booming oil, steel and railroad industries. In fact, it was these booming industries that eventually transformed the US in to a superpower. But 'all that glitters is not gold.

Under the glitter of the wealth, the complete economic and political system was corrupt and huge income inequalities existed in the society. After all wealth (and that means real wealth not just pieces of paper) in this universe is finite and unless someone gets poorer, the other person cannot become rich. Any change to make a person better off is impossible without making someone worse off and in that era, there were woefully few people who were better off and a huge mass of population was worse off. The situation became acute during the great depression. We might be again revisiting that era. At least the signs are ominous enough.

The Federal Reserve Boards' Survey of Consumer Finance explicitly furnishes this point. In the present situation, the top 1 percent of the American population owns more than 33 percent of all the wealth of the United States and 50 percent of the population, i.e. half of the total American population survives on a meager 2.5 percent. And that is not the end. The lions' share have been increasing at a steady rate in the past few decades, while the share o the pie for half the population have been decreasing continuously. And with the recession on top, this division is poised to grow only larger as time goes by.

And the rich this time is not just a few American industrialists. For example, in 2006, the collective income of the top 25 hedge fund managers of the US stood at a staggering $14 billion. This amount would approximately equate the earnings of almost a million middle class families, accumulated over a period of three years. Most of the top rich in the US consists of people working in the financial sector. However, this does not mean that the sole reason of disparity is economics. It is also closely related to politics because it is political decisions that define the distribution of income and as we have seen in our history, the rich also needs political support to make them richer.

However, the interesting point is, there has never been a political backlash from the people towards a government that prefers the rich at the common American's expense. Since the period of Cold War, tax cuts for the rich, busting of union organisations and politics that turn a blind eye towards the business interests of the rich have extended the gap between the haves and the have nots to a large extent. For a recent example, America can afford to cut jobs and pensions, but when it comes to get their rich friends like Merrill Lynch or Fannie Mae out of trouble, there is no compromise. In the pretext of getting them out of trouble, the US will spend as much as necessary to make its rich friends richer at the expense of rising debts and inflation. And these are not runaway incidents. When the government talks of tax-breaks, it is referring breaks only for the rich. Incredible as it may sound, about two thirds of the benefits from tax cuts between the period of 2001 and 2003 went to the people residing prettily on the top fifth of the income segment. One may ask how much poverty they are facing to deserve the major chunk of tax benefits. Many low-income household do not receive tax refunds. However, due to the enormous loss of revenue at the top, there were huge budget deficits and the government had cut social programmes such as financial aid and Medicare.

In most cases, when a tax cut happens, it is not meant for the people who make under a million dollar a year. Some of the government's tax cuts are simply irrelevant as far as the middle and the lower middle class are concerned. For example, people with lower incomes or do not benefit from dividend tax breaks just because they do not have any money that can be invested in bonds and stocks. It will not be much of a surprise to know that almost half of such tax breaks went to people who made over a million dollar a year. This is where people such as the hedge fund managers make money – through tax breaks and through exploiting tax loopholes. Although these hedge fund managers are taxed at the rate of 35 percent, much of their income is considered as capital gains – a small exploitable loophole devised, developed and exploited by the rich – and these people are actually taxed at a rate of 15 percent. It has been estimated that $6 billion had been lost in 2006-07 due to such privileges enjoyed by them. Out of the $6 billion, $2 billion went to only 25 hedge fund managers. Therefore the American economic system is inherently designed to increase the riches of the privileged class, which in turn increases income disparity.

Although the working class in the US are facing innumerable problems such as increasing health insurance costs and no savings for retirement due to volatile markets, they cannot go to the unions, which are responsible for taking up such issues as healthcare and fair wage to voice the deprived worker class. This is because their numbers have been made to decline steadily since the 70s. Even home ownership, which at one point of time was considered as the identity of the American middle class, is gradually becoming a distant dream to this segment due to the subprime crisis.

It would be interesting to note that the recession is taking place at a moment of history where deterioration of US as a superpower is the most significant characteristic. The impact of the recession will therefore be multiplied gradually transforming the recession in to a depression. The great US consumer is now defaulting as he cannot borrow any more money and consumer insolvency would be a key factor to turn the recession in to a depression. Retail and manufacturing segments will slow down considerably enhanced by the fact that employment has already been hit and after real estate and construction, it is now the turn of the retail and manufacturing to take the legacy of layoffs forward. This trend will soon be picked up by the other sectors of the society.

Without salaries to sustain themselves and their families and without credit (and already such signs are showing), the American middle class can no longer consume what it was consuming a decade back. Almost 70% of the growth of US depended on domestic consumption and once the consumption is hit, growth will take a death blow. As consumers withdraw from markets, first the business houses depending directly on consumers will be affected. These negative tends will eventually spread like a cancer to other sectors. The US financial sector, already reeling under the consequences of the subprime crisis and buried under mounting debts will be in the eye of the storm. The whole process will go into a negative loop or a vicious circle. Since the companies will witness a decline in their profits, they will try to stay afloat by cutting down on employees resulting in more unemployment. More unemployment will mean that people will earn less and thus their consumption will go down. As consumption decreases, companies will be able to sell less, which in turn will decrease their profits.

In the international market, terms of trade will shift away from the US. The Euro Dollar exchange rate is shifting. And as more and more nations such as China witness the US economy going into a recession, they will accelerate a drop in capital flows invested, and will aggravate the trade deficit of US. Such a situation will lead to a decline in the value of the UD dollar as against other currencies of the world; increasing imported inflation and increasing trade tensions between the US and its trading partners such as China and Japan. Both these countries will see a fall in their export profits as majority of their exports are imports for the US. In fact stockpiling has begun in Japan as a backlash of the recession in US with inventories building up in various products. On the other hand, US have very few alternatives to export and therefore its trade deficit is not going to get any better.

However, a recession in US will greatly affect its trading partners – especially China – and it would be interesting to see how the country reacts to such a huge loss in exports. The US Federal Reserve will have to answer a few questions. After amassing huge debts, and continuously inflating the economy with money supply, what did the Federal Reserve wait till the country got into recession before reducing the rates of interest? This will be the question that will probably land the Fed at the centre of a political, economic and financial turmoil. The Fed will also remain clueless till the bubble bursts in the economy and the value of the dollar hits the rock bottom. The value of the dollar, and how far it will fall will aging be dependent on two basic premises: whether any belief still exists in the intrinsic value of the economy and the dollar, and the level of the interest rates favourable to the economy. But more and more nations are showing their mistrust in the US dollar and therefore, interest rate is the only likely friend that can try to prevent the collapse of the economy.

However, the catch is, if Fed declares that only interest rates can be used to try and save the economy, in other words it would be saying that the US dollar has lost all its value, and thereby bring in a faster and more rapid collapse of the dollar. Therefore it would come down to a trade off between salvaging whatever value the dollar is left with at a cost of more people losing jobs with their pension funds being wiped clean due to a falling market.

Since US is the epicentre of the global economic meltdown, the impact here is being felt like nowhere else. The burst of the housing bubble has impoverished millions of Americans. And incidentally, each month, the foreclosures are being doubled. As a result millions of people have literally come on to the street or are trying to find homes at poorer locales. Just like official statistics had denied the housing bubble or the subprime crisis in previous occasions, it is now playing down the fact that millions of Americans are losing jobs. Ironically, there were many US households who used to use the house mortgage to finance their livelihood. These people have been one of the worst hit in the housing slump as they had to come down on their standard of living immediately after the housing bubble burst. Some of them is still running on whatever other savings they had accumulated, and after the savings is depleted, they will have to look for other options.

Public services are on an all time low streak for lack of sufficient income. The huge amount of money borrowed and spent by the Bush administration is taking its toll on the Americans by denying them the different public services scheme. Some economists feel that, politics aside, there is something intrinsically wrong with the nation that refuses to provide healthcare to the public, and spends the money instead on financing wars. In fact, the army and other defence forces in the US seem to be the only government segment with credibility. Millions of Americans depend on the military for their livelihood.

Trade Deficits

To understand where the crisis is going to go from its present situation, a lot of people will be keeping an eye on the figures of the US trade deficit. With a deficit of $707 dollars, which approximately equals to 5% of GDP at an annual rate, it is astonishing to note how much money the US owes to the world. The trade deficit had actually peaked at $800 billion in 2006. Most economists are of the opinion that the economic crisis is a direct result of America's mountain of debts and huge consumption. Giant mortgages have left homeowners in disarray, markets are flat, and the US is facing the greatest depression since the Great Depression of the 30s. Still America keeps borrowing and maintains a humungous trade deficit. Some things never change, do they? Still the question arises: how long can America keep such high deficits?

From here onwards, either the deficits can remain where they are and in fact increase if the world continues to have faith in the dollar, keeps shipping goods to the US and continues to lend money to America for the imports. Or, the US consumers cut back on consumption and as a result, trade deficit shrinks and international trade adjusts itself at the equilibrium. However, trade deficit can also shrink as the US exports more goods and services to the world.

The global economic boom that had been witnessed by countries in the past decade have been mostly due to large multinational corporates shipping technology and business knowledge to countries such as India, China and many of the other South East Asian countries; and in return of the flow of this knowledge, the developed economies, and especially the US got back truckloads of cheap labour and services from these countries. Since the year 2000, the US borrowed approximately an astounding figure of $5 trillion from the world to finance these imports.

Out of this $5 trillion, the government borrowed approximately $1.5 trillion directly from overseas. However, most of the borrowing was routed through the Wall Street in the form of bonds, equities and securities. The firms of Wall Street played middle men between the world and the US consumers. That was specifically the reason what the Wall Street boomed in the recent times. The hedge fund managers minted foreign money as it came to the US through them and they became rich. However, when the global economy understood that the US consumers cannot carry any more burdens of loans on their shoulders, the turned off the tap of financial inflow into the US. This is one reason why the global boom stopped abruptly and financial crisis took its place.

Now, in the present scenario, if the government wants to open up the tap from the global economy again, it will have to take up what the US consumers were doing – borrow money from outside. If the government delivers a massive fiscal stimulus, the deficit will stay high, the companies can keep outsourcing production and the inflow of money can be resumed. Only, now the money will go through Washington and not Wall Street. So everything will be as they were before; at least for a while.

However, the catch over here is: the government will have to keep mounting on debts, on top of whatever mountains they have already created. But such huge debts got the US into trouble on the first place. And since the government will borrow, the US economy will have to be pledged. And this debt will keep on piling till there is a bubble burst and then let the economy correct itself. However this scenario means the middle class will be hurt. With such huge debts on their heads and inflation running high due to government borrowing, they will not have many a places to run to.

In the second case, the US consumers cut back on imports and the trade deficits shrink. But in this case, the government stays back and not ward off a deep recession with monetary stimulus. The recession will go deep and acute and the dollar will fall until it hits the rock bottom. This is the natural course of the events. However, this process will hurt most economies in the short run. With no cheap imports, living standards will shrink and middle class will be hard squeezed as there will be massive job cuts, especially in segments that depend on foreign products as inputs. Countries such as China and Japan that excessively depends on the US to sell their goods will also have to adjust to the situation as there will be excess supply in these markets without foreign demand.

However, since the dollar will fall, there will be chaos in the domestic economy and people who saved money in dollars will be in dire straits. The government will also have to look forward to go back to the basics and back up the dollar with gold. Restructuring the whole economy will take time, but it will give the economy a chance to start afresh.

In the third case, the US starts producing more innovative and technologically enhanced products and starts exporting them, bringing down the trade deficit over a period of time. However, the problem here is till there is some major technological advancement or breakthrough, the US government have to keep piling debt upon debt and hope that the domestic market comes out soon with products that can me exported. This scenario though sounds better than the other two would be highly improbable to apply as it would mean staying put for an indefinite period of time.

In any case, due to the high debts and huge trade deficits, the middle class will get squeezed – probably to the extent as last witnessed in the Great Depression. The best people can do is guard themselves against volatility by investing in the right things and planning out their financials well.

Capitalism or Socialism

When markets are on a roll and sky scrapping like Manhattan, capitalism seems so dear but when things go wrong, markets do not bad an eye lid before cuddling up to socialism. That seems to be the story or the Great American Trick of our markets. After all the Federal Reserve has to take care of its friends in the Wall Street or they may whine about being orphaned.

That explains the mammoth credit bubble created by the successive regimes whereby they pumped in huge capital in the market to tide over temporarily. The banks have always been in bed with the government bringing in their own ways of financial re-engineering to suit the market. Money attracts money, borrowing fuels more borrowing, demand goes up and value of financial assets goes on a spiraling upward journey. As per some estimates, major banks have reported losses of nearly $ 45 billion on their investments. To add to it, assets valued at almost a trillion dollars are finding its way back into the balance sheets of banks as collateral debt obligations. How does the Federal Reserve react to such a situation? It is simple; they just cut the interest rates. Any economist with a sane mind would point out that lower cuts are not consistent with inflation levels resulting from higher prices of crude oil, escalating food prices, the inflationary effect of a weakening dollar and increasing pressure mounted by emerging economies such as India and China. The stratagem of the US Central Bank is crystal clear. To tide over the credit bubble crisis, there needs to be a substantial cut in the quantum of borrowings and control of the global financial systems. The augmentation of the prices of assets brought about by the excessive borrowing by the government and banks needs to be corrected. For only a correction of the market will quell the situation or else banks would destabilize irrevocably.

Alternatively, the de-leveraging and price adjustment can be achieved by creating inflation through a loose monetary policy. Assuming that the prices of assets remain at the existing levels, a higher inflation would cause values of rentals to fall alternatively steeper inflation would cut down the value of borrowings that need to be paid back thus allowing the required reduction in leverage.

For instance, during 1960 to 1975, the Dow Jones Industrial Average remained significantly unchanged. This is the calls to reverse the policy. Back then, if inflation averaged 5 per cent per annum, then the value of the market (without taking dividends into account) lost about 50

% of its value in inflation terms. The policy of the Federal Reserve has helped affected banks.

Writing down of risky assets by the government means that such banks need large intake of capital. Taking into account the recent performance and restrained profits, it would be difficult for these banks to raise this much needed capital at satisfactory prices. Banks can borrow cheaply when interest rates are low and the monies gotten from such borrowing can be used to buy government bonds that provide higher returns than the cost of borrowing. This produces profits for the bank without them having to hold capital against their assets. This as a bank is generally not required to hold capital against government securities. In all this process, banks get revitalized and also get the much needed capital to work with.

The government of America has a trick up its sleeve as constitutionally fund its large deficit by selling off its debt to the banks. This move can be considered in a scenario where demand for the US dollar slides heavily due to its steep fall. Such a move would not be a first of its kind as Japan has already used such a technique exactly two decades ago.

Expectations of inflation rising further are by now prevalent in the market as shown as rising gold prices and a dollar that is weakening by the day. As is common during high inflation or expectations of one, investment funds particularly foreign shift from investing in bonds to investing in real estate. While higher inflation means rental values fall down, value of real estate per se goes up. Now the real downside of this entire process: inflation can potentially cause transfer of wealth from those who are investing to those who are borrowing. What then happens to the middle class is the big question on everyone's minds.

A brave and dangerous move of the Federal Reserve to up the interest rates to flush out inflation out of the system can also have undesired results as liquidity of the market may not improve. But then lower interest rates may set off bubbles like the credit bubble. So to be fair to the government and the Federal Reserve, they have limited options to pull themselves out of this state of affairs.

Like they say a government cannot privatize profits and socialize losses. But that seems to be the mantra of the financial markets.

THE SHRINKAGE OF MIDDLE CLASS IN THE U.S.

The shrinkage is contested by the intelligentsia that has chosen to gauge the nerve of the middle class in diverse stipulations, be it by altering the income brackets or centering on job groups. While some scholars see little or no shrinkage at all, a lot of them are convinced that the shrinkage is for real. But the moot point is that whatever way one looks it at, there always crops up a phenomena.

However, any method of quantification of the middle class necessitates drawing random brackets, both economic and psychological, around the middle class. At least a few of the economists think this is a wrong way to be looking at things in perspective.

The dismissive side of the middle class mass departure has had many neo liberal thinking experts up in arms. Their perspective is that the shift in the American economy from unionized, factory work to service-industry professions has brought a substantial loss of jobs to the middle class. Traditionally, the blue-collar jobs have tended to be plagued with unions while on the other hand the new service industries typically offer neither such wage nor any job protection.

The case in point is that all this time some, if not all, sections of the middle class were afforded inherent job that has now been shattered. Many middle class employees lost out in the economic slump as they were conceived to be of skills that can be done away with. Ben Jones of Louisiana coast was supporting his wife and their two children at ease with his $ 34,000 pay working at an oil rig when the slowdown in his sector hit him costing his job. *"I am now shifting from here and intend to take up a job with 30 % to 40 % pay cut. It is stupid to think, people will continue to earn what they used to before the recession,"* he says.

According to experts, single parents are adding to the woes of the low income groups. This as often unmarried mothers and divorcees from middle income families often slip into the lower income class when they try to get by on their own. The reasons for this slide are many, the primary reason being that they now have to endure the double burden of child care on the back of lack of skills needed in job market.

Cameroon Harvey, 33, of Detroit, earns $ 15,000 as a junior level accountant, along with federal food assistance. The unwed mother of a two-year-old daughter, she has to spend $ 220 a month for day care, which eats up nearly 25 % of her net income. To make up money for meeting her rent, she is sharing her room with her brother, Sam, a factory worker. It is mentioned here that not all observers believe the middle class is being seriously shrinking. They cite that there is a lack of polarization and also there experience of observing the trends as seen in the early 1970s and 1980s when there was a spurt in the number of the middle and upper class workers and a fall in the number of low income groups. It must be noted here that this analysis is bereft of the process of matching some displaced workers to the new middle-class jobs that are being created.

For instance if a job in the automotive sector in Detroit is replaced by a job in the insurance sector in New York with the same pay packet, the distribution of income may not change but the life of the person definitely will. The other view is that though the size of middle class income may have been pinched a little but they are factors that are temporary in nature. Then there is the flood of young baby boomers into the job market that also needs to be taken into cognizance as these baby boomers are being held responsible for bringing about a dip in the incomes of the middle class. The only silver lining though is that as bulk of these baby boomers were in entry level jobs, they brought down the overall average but with time their income is expected to go up bringing about the necessary correction.

Notwithstanding such comments and observations, an average middle class family is the US still feels that they are indeed dipping below their earlier standards of living. The very basic needs that middle class Americans were earlier finding easy to fulfill like their own house, schooling and college education for their kids and family vacations are gradually getting out of their reach. The happier times for the middle class America were between 1950 and 1960 till the ride came to a grinding halt due to the vertical rise of inflation in the early 1970s. This is what experts categorize as middle class blues with an ever looming threat of downward mobility and a constant fear of a slide in their economic stability which was enjoyed by their preceding generations. Says Jacob Carvalho, 34, an IT administrator settled in New Jersey, "*I always feel that my dad was able to perform better professionally in lesser number of years. I will have to work twice as hard and put in double the number of years to get to where he reached."*

This points out that many people who chose typical middle class careers are not happy with their economic standing and fear a slump in the social and economic position that will drive them to being a lower class family. Putting aside all the theories about the real shrinkage of the middle class, even if the shrinkage is in the minds of middle class American families, it still is a matter of grave concern for the country. The disappearance of the middle class would mean that a large bloc of culturally, politically aware citizenry which served as the backbone for any major political or economic decisions of successive US governments is no more and the political class would be left to fend for themselves caught between the haves and have-nots without any unanimity or consensus being reached regarding any important political or economic policies of the state. The shrinkage of the middle class should by this yardstick concern the administration more than it does the million of American middle class families themselves.

Those favoring the polarization theory say that such a process has already been set in motion in the business sectors like retail. The retailing industry is now clearly looking at upscale markets and consumers who can termed as the elitist. And this change in mindsets of business houses is not just restricted to the retail sector as even food, clothing industry are going in a change of approach and products keeping in mind not the middle class but the upper classes. The result of such polarization of society, she warns, could be a warping of the country's identity. Such a shift could further the polarization that has already been set in motion even if it considered only in the minds of middle class America. Analysts say that government should strictly stem the follow of jobs with fat salaries outside the country so that the American middle class is not denied its pound of flesh in the job market. The government needs to come to the rescue of workers like Ben Jones and ensure that his skills do not become unwanted in the job market. America cannot afford to lose its Ben Jones and its middle class lest it will be plunged into a quagmire out which extrication would be next to impossible.

WHAT WILL THE GOVERNMENT DO?

When it comes to a tradeoff between the precarious financial system existing in the home markets where the Americans have already been over-stretched, and the US's ability to finance and resolve the humongous debt that it has accumulated over the years, the decision of the US policy makers seemed pretty obvious in the minds of most economists.

Everything and anything can be sacrificed by the US policy makers in order to protect the nation's ability to borrow abroad. After all that is what America is all about. Without the ability to borrow, the government cannot conduct its wars of aggression, and the Americans cannot continue to consume $800 billion dollars more than the economy produces on a yearly basis.

One does not have to look too far. Just a few years ago the euro was trading against 85 cents of America. At present it is worth $1.48. Such a comparison reveals how rapidly the dollar is losing its value. Other nations that finance the US budget and trade deficits, have been experiencing a huge drop in the value of their dollar holdings. Gradually the confidence erodes away, until one day they will decide that they had enough of the dollars. The interest rate applied on the US Treasury bonds does not even come close to compensating these foreign nations for the decline in the value of the dollar against other currencies. On the other hand, even the returns on investment from real estate and equities; do not offset the losses from the decline in the dollar's value.

China and Japan together holds almost two trillion American dollars. However, most of their holdings are in the form of American assets. Other countries have lesser but nevertheless, substantial amounts of US dollars. As the dollar is reserve currency, the entire world's investment is inflated in dollars.

However, no country wants to hold an asset that is continuously depreciating in value, and no country wants to acquire more of such assets. According to Wall Street, foreign countries are accumulating US dollars so as to protect the value of their existing dollar holdings. However, according to statistics, the US dollar has lost more than 60% of its value in this decade. This goes against the theory of Wall Street that foreign countries are hooked on to US dollars.

The dollar would have completely collapsed by this time had there been anything else to replace it as reserve currency. Compared to the dollar, the euro is the monetary unit of the European Union. But the countries of Europe have not surrendered to the EU. And the United Kingdom still retains the British pound. Technically, the euro can rise in value many times higher than those of the dollar.

The sole purpose of Japan and China to accumulate dollars is to increase their penetration and capture the super-consuming domestic market of the US. Both these countries have increased the productive capacity of their industrial sector. The wealth created in their domestic economies by exporting finished goods to the US is a compensation for the decline in the value of dollar holdings. However, both China and Japan have seen the writing on the wall, and whatever the Fed and the Wall Street may do to hide it, the fact remains: By offshoring production, the US has can no way close, or even decrease its trade deficit to a considerable extent. The offshored produce of US firms is regarded as imports when they return to the US to be marketed in the domestic economy. The more US production moves abroad, the less there is to export. In comparison to this, imports seem to rise widening its trade deficit.

Gradually, the entire world is realizing that they cannot continue to give the Americans goods and services in exchange for depreciating paper dollars for an infinite period of time. China is turning its development inward and is beginning to rely on its potentially huge domestic market. Japan, on the other hand, is pinning its hopes on the emerging markets of Asia.

The day foreign nations stop accumulating US dollars, the dollar will be reduced to what it really is – fake money. And the day foreign nations were to dump or reduce their existing holdings of dollars, superpower USA will disappear instantly. However, foreign countries are still accumulating dollars, though at a considerable lower rate. New dollars are still being churned out at high rates decreasing their value.

These foreign nations have continued to accumulate US dollars with the hope that sooner or later the nation will address its trade and budget deficits. The bad news is these deficits have passed the point of no return.

The sharp decline in the dollar, as one may expect, should have closed the trade deficit by increasing exports and decreasing imports to maintain a balance. However, offshoring prevents the possibility of exports reducing the trade deficit as American goods consumed by the Americans are being produced abroad and are returning as imported goods in the US. And now, the Americans are now dependent on imports, for which there exists no domestically produced alternatives. The US trade deficit will close by itself when foreign countries cease to finance it. However, such a situation may mean that many of the middle and the lower middle class citizens may die of hunger since America will not be able to take care of them.

If the budget deficit is attempted to be closed by taxation, unemployment and poverty will go through the roof. American median family incomes have been almost stagnating in the 21st century. If the huge bonuses, paid to CEOs for offshoring, and to Wall Street for marketing subprime derivatives are removed from these figures, Americans have actually experienced a decline in real income.

The situation may be direr than is thought of. According to some of the recent studies, many of the US statistical data systems were set in place prior to the advent of offshoring. These data have been counting foreign production as part of US productivity and GDP growth, thus inflating the real performance of the US economy.

The falling dollar has pushed up oil prices to $100 a barrel. When the price of a commodity such as oil increases, it creates inflation in the economy as their price rise drives up the prices of other essential commodities. The price rise becomes a horizontal one while the middle class suffers as they remain where they were before the rise. The falling dollar also means that the imports, on which Americans are dependent, will rise in price.

In the 21st century, the US economy has been boosted by consumers who spend more than they can earn. Massive consumption, fueled by rises in indebtedness, received its greatest boost from the Federal Reserve's low interest rate policy. Greenspan successfully covered up the effects of offshoring on the economy by engineering a housing bubble. Such a bubble created employment in the construction and financial firms and pushed up home prices. The fallacy of the situation is the US government made consumers spends to create consumer demand.

However, bubbles always burst. And the payment for the shortsightedness of American policy makers always falls on the shoulders of the common people. The full consequences of the housing bubble bust are not yet fully realized.

ARE THE MIDDLE CLASS LEARNING FROM THIS MESS?

If one asks an outsider, a layman, a formula for America to pull itself out its self created financial mess, possibly the response would be, *"They should throw away their credit cars and buy less of land rovers."* Quite a possible suggestion, one should imagine. So, why don't we Americans throw away our credit cards, stopping buying SUVs, spending on exotic vacations and cruises abroad? Become more prudent, or put it more euphemistically, become penny-wise. Well, there is a theory doing the rounds (mind you it is not another conspiracy theory) that prudence has also crept into our middle class and people may not exactly be throwing up their credit cards but are definitely looking to close them what with lucrative credit closing offers that banks are coming up with. There are such stories of middle class becoming penny-wise in America. And a few experiences may be worth recounting.

A family of five in Washington that resides in a palatial bungalow has become a point of curiosity for the neighborhood as they have suddenly become penny-wise. The kids, all teenagers prefer to walk closer destinations; do not believe in shopping frequently, they use tap water at home, switch off their television when nobody is seriously watching. No, they are not victims of the recession that has clouded America they just chose to become penny-wise before they have none to save. Their parents, Bill Paxton and Annie Paxton are employed with god salaries and believe it or not, they do not have any credit card outstanding. It was always considered to be patriotic to spend more in America. Not any longer. Some American middle class families are learning to change and change to suit the crisis that has engulfed their country and affected thousands of middle class families.

Such sea change was only witnessed during the Great Depression when Americans changed their ways of life but after that it was back to square one. Consumption has always been the pillar of our society. Can an American go without credit cards? Yes, many middle class families do believe in this.

Such harbingers of middle class families who hitherto over consumed during the last one decade are now indulging in introspection of their spendthrift ways of living be it due to fears of getting a pink slip at workplace or shocked due to investment losses or just plain lack of understanding of the tumbling of the markets. Not surprising though considering the fact that the current financial crisis is something that is on par with the 1930s when American consumers actually changed their way of life. Not everybody is welcoming it, as it is also being resented by many families that do not want to change. That people are turning penny-wise is proven and backed by solid data, data that shows that personal consumption is falling in the US for the first time in the last two decades.

Some analysts believe that anyway consumers will not be in a position to spend freely like before for at least the next five years. So it makes sense to be prudent and save one's family. The American middle class families cannot by any stretch of imagination save the economy but the least they can do is to save themselves from falling into personal debt traps any further. Consumption has always been a part of the American psyche. But the major break in customary trends started in the early 1990s when the country and its peoples started consuming more than that was being produced. Most of this consumption was financed by debt. People consumed more because of easy and some may say cheap debt. It is interesting to note that in terms of consumer debt, US had a relatively stable period from 1940 to 1970 which means an entire generation with only marginal growth in consumer credit. It is pertinent here to take a look at the history of credit cards in the US. Credit cards started making a push in the 1950s with Diners Club and American Express which was then followed by big names like Visa. And from that point onwards Americans have been using credit cards taking the amount of credit card debt alone to unimaginable figures. And now people just did not shop with their credit cards but started even off installments on cars with their credit cards. What they need to do now is to reach into their wallets again to spend with greenbacks and not plastic money.

Frugality perhaps went of the system and out of style since the founding of the republic. This is in sharp contrast to people who lived through the Great Depression and in some cases were marked for life by the experience. Typical of them is Robert Lim, an 84-year-old resident of New York who grew up poor in the Bronx. In the early 1930s, his father lost heavily on his grocery store after which it took him eight years before he could land with a decent job. Even now, Lim despite his riches, shops for food armed with coupons cut from the papers and takes the subway rather than taxis. It shows that important lessons he learnt but did not forget. Lim's baby boomer children grew up without psychological scars from the Depression but have been brought up in the age of consumption, easily available credit cards and the era of SUVs. So then, the sudden need for prudence comes as rude awakening to them. And that is fix that is being faced by several middle class and upper middle class families.

This is where there is a need to bring about the culture of being penny-wise and adopting thriftier lifestyles. The urge to go on a shopping spree or buy to keep buying fancy mobile phones can easily be controlled. Small measures help save big bucks.

Also contributing to the new spate of penny-pinching are widespread concerns about how much longer the recession will last. Well over 70 %of Americans expect the downturn to last for at least one year while a third think it will last for another two to three years. It is these people who see an extended recession that are more likely to cut down on their buying habits. It is a crucial thing to understand for the rest of America and also the government as roughly 70 % of the Gross Domestic Product is based on consumption. So, one need to listen to what the consumer is saying. The loss of jobs has meant that several American families have changed their patterns of consumption.

Things nearly spun out of control for the Herberts living in Cleveland, Texas, after they upgraded to a better and bigger house. Despite wiping off their retirement funds to help with the down payment, they ended up with higher monthly payments. Two years ago, they sold their previous home only to realize that it would take away only $ 65,000 even though the place had nearly doubled in value. They then decided live more prudently. No more cruises or expensive vacations. They told their kids that they would get an allowance of only $ 25 per month and that they would be walking to their school, the local store, and even to their friends' houses.

The kids, Ann and John, were intrigued at first as they felt that their comfortable, materialistic lives were drastically changing. Bob Herbert who himself was addicted to shopping found it difficult to control himself but later adjusted well. And on the rare occasions the Herberts do go out to dinner, they feel guilty. Since making their big changes, they accelerated payments on their car loan and managed to pay it off. To bring about such a change within oneself, there are many things to take note of. "One is to be flexible: Give yourself a treat every now and then. Another is to have a goal. Being frugal is like dieting. It is more sustainable if you have a target you are aiming for," say the Herberts.

As joblessness creeps up, many more Americans will receive their own crash course in frugality. It has already happened to Ted Doherty, 54, a salesman who lives in New York. He recently got a new job, took a pay cut and has been living prudently ever since. Doherty says he is in it for the long haul willing to spend more up front to enjoy the benefits of these savings over the following years. He installed expensive but energy saving CFL light bulbs in his house, and replaced some of his electronic appliances with more efficient ones. For him, every cent counts. Like a lot of baby boomers, Doherty has a nest egg, but many people in their 20s and 30s have little to fall back on.

To fall in line, they have to learn the difference between necessities and discretionary spending. In the past, consumers have gone shopping the moment things became hunky dory. But will that happen again this time? That is something that is for the researchers to find out. Let us hope that Americans will after throw away their credit cards and not buy SUVs but shift to smaller cars like middle class families in India and China.

So, is the American customer transformed forever? Did the existing downturn vary the ostensibly inexorable spending maniac known as the American customer? From early hints, it looks like some behaviors will be changed for a very long time to come. This is a drastic departure given the nearly infinite round of crises in the last three decades concluding with the dramatically frenzied housing crisis. But many Americans are now feeling the credit withdrawal trouble. For most, the never-ending stream of credit card offers has turned into a dribble and in many cases, a complete famine. Much of this is being brought about by a new found asceticism and even shunning of consumption.

In a recent Gallup survey, it was found that 48 %of Americans making $ 60,000 or less would be unable to make a big purchase if they had to. 20 % making less than $ 24,000 followed them.

What this is means is that 50 % of US households are making $ 50,000 or less. When one sifts through data like this there is an understanding of the motivation for massive incentives. It is interesting to note that, several people when asked in that survey if they have enough money to buy the things they need said that they did have that money.

In these times, wants are completely far off from needs. This could mean that far more Americans are finding a completely new respect for their jobs particularly in the light of the 26 million unemployed and underemployed in the country. Savings is in, at least for a few. As mentioned earlier, retail sales have fallen and hence the change in strategy of this industry. The days of the bubble are gone and people now tend to spend with more caution if nothing. Also, the unemployed are also finding it tough to get back into jobs.

It does not help matters that major corporations in the country are not hiring in large numbers. This even as the number of lay-offs has actually come down. These unemployed are critical aspects of the entire population. Their consumption levels have fallen off the cliff and income levels at an all time low. In hindsight, it is now easier to understand why American consumers behaved the way they did in the last few decades. That they depended on the bubbles is quite clear.

Even with all stimulus packages, an average employee in the US is still finding it difficult to live the way he or she did before the slump. This should surprise all those who had predicted that consumption read spending would return to normalcy in the months to come. People making such predictions should also note that most baby boomers that are nearing retirement are looking for savings than consumption given the present market scenario. It is a paradox for these baby boomers as the wealth they created may not be theirs to enjoy. If this is the situation of the baby boomers, then what happens to those in their early 20s and 30s trying to save their selves from this economic downturn? Well, they could look to become penny-wise.

While talking the importance of becoming penny-wise, it is pertinent to find out the current earnings of an average American middle class family. The answers to these questions could also help us in going about resolving the present financial crisis in a more organized and scientific method. It also makes all the more sense as most of the middle class not just in the US but in other countries are mostly losing money and not making more. According to some estimates, the median household earnings in the country are about $ 46,000. This effectively means that about half the American population has to make do with $ 46,000 per annum or even less than that. Even at this point of time, the entire suggested panacea to get out of this economic downturn is failing to focus on the income and employment aspect which is really sad. The government needs to take a re-look at this aspect. As per estimates, a mere 17 % of all American households make more than nearly $ 120,000 per annum. An estimated 2.7 % earn more than $ 200,000.

The reality that only 34 % of the people earn more than $65,000 is amazing given how costly other basic expenditures have gotten over the last 10 years. This is exactly why middle class is feeling pinched and analysts are talking about shrinkage of the middle class. If one tries putting together a budget for a family earning $ 100,000, things will fall into perspective.

What is even more enthralling, is how even among the super rich, income is not circulated uniformly. There are roughly 146,000 (0.1%) households with incomes beyond $ 1,500,000 per annum. Even at that, the top 0.01% of households had incomes of $ 5,500,000 and accounted for 11,000 households. The first 400 highest tax payers in America together earned a whopping $ 87,000,000 per annum. That definitely is wealth.

For ordinary mortals, $46,000 does not go a long way. As per the recent census figures, there are 110,000,000 households in the country. What this data shows is that 55,000,000 households are making $ 46,000 or even less in a year. Many a families now cannot even think about pre-retirement savings. In light of the recent tumbles in the stock market and en estimated loss of $ 50 trillion of wealth world over, one wonders what lies in store ahead. The bottom line is the middle class families in the US are pushed into a corner in every conceivable way. For the government, perhaps they should be focusing more on the employment and income levels of the middle class than bailing out banks and automobile companies. While the stimulus package is some good news for the industry, American middle class families are left to wonder who is going to come to their rescue.

LATEST FIGURES AND LATEST SITUATIONS

What you're witnessing in the U.S. today is not a health care debate. It's a health care WAR. But it's too soon to take sides: Neither has defined its territory; both are escalating the battle with weapons of mass disgrace.

In the meantime, millions of Americans are potentially innocent victims of the collateral damage — both financially and physically.

But if you're among those upset at the Obama administration for trying to ram through a health reform bill, wait till you see what most health insurance companies are doing — and have been doing for many years!

- They routinely overcharge you on premiums when you're healthy and deny your claims when you're sick.
- They welcome your policy when you don't need it and shred it when you do.
- Adding financial insult to personal injury, they take the savings you've worked so hard to earn and throw it into high-risk investments you'd never touch with a ten-foot pole.

Most health insurers spend substantial sums in order to

- develop computer programs and systems that automatically and repeatedly deny and delay claims payments;
- hire doctors specialized in poking holes in legitimate claims; and
- give extra bonuses to employees who can successfully deny the most claims.

In sum, health insurers build massive machines designed with the sole purpose of denying and delaying your claims.

They know that few policyholders will take legal action. Plus, even though policyholders do win judgments, the companies can earn a lot of extra income on the funds they hold back with delayed claims payments. *The longer you or your doctor has to wait for reimbursement, the more income they can make on your money.*

And unfortunately, this is not just about a few bad apples in the industry. According to the National Association of Insurance Commissioners (NAIC), in 2008 alone, policyholders filed 195,669 complaints against insurance companies. That *excludes* complaints in many states which do not compile comparable data and, needless to say, it also excludes the millions of Americans who do not file a formal complaint.

The two most common types of complaints of all: delays and denials.

"All too often," says New York Attorney General Cuomo, "insurers play a game of deny, delay, and deceive." And, I might add, all too often, people are bankrupted by the expenses or die waiting for the care.

But it gets worse...

Just last Tuesday, the U.S. Department of Health and Human Services released a study demonstrating that, in most states:

- Insurance companies can retroactively cancel individual policies if *any* condition was not disclosed when the policy was obtained. More to the point, insurers can cancel the policies *even if the medical condition is unrelated and even if the person was not aware of the condition at the time.* (Italics are mine.)
- Coverage can also be revoked for all members of a family, even if only one family member failed to disclose a medical condition.

And again, companies institute sophisticated systems and procedures that maximize the savings with these underhanded tactics, including special compensations for employees who can deploy them most effectively.

Two major insurers have admitted to Congressional committees that they automatically investigate the medical records of every policyholder with certain conditions, including leukemia, ovarian cancer, brain cancer, and becoming pregnant with twins.

For example, in one case, after a Texas resident was found to have a lump in her breast, the insurance company investigated her medical history and concluded that she had been diagnosed previously with osteoporosis. Although that condition was unrelated to breast cancer, the company used it as an excuse to cancel her policy.

No, I don't support the notion that underwriting — the process of denying coverage or charging higher premiums due to *known* risks — is somehow evil.

Quite the contrary, if insurers do NOT protect themselves from those risks, they may not be financially capable of fulfilling their promises to all other policyholders. But systematically leveraging contract loopholes to cancel policies *after* a condition is diagnosed fails to pass the most basic of smell tests.

The most insidious abuse of all:
Direct interference with medically recommended procedures

...

"One of our big frustrations with insurance companies," says GOP Congressman Tim Murphy, "is they control the market place, they control what's done," and what doctors decide.

Indeed, in 50 out of 300 U.S. metropolitan areas, a single health insurer controls at least 70 percent of customers. And in many more areas, just *two* health insurance companies dominate the market.

That puts both you and your doctor at a great disadvantage.

End result: Your doctor's decisions about what's best for *your* health are frequently overruled by the insurer's decisions about what's best for *its* bottom line.

Most patients don't realize how widespread this is and how deeply it can impact the quality of care. Most doctors, meanwhile, are so sick and tired of insurance company interference, they've given up complaining.

On September 10, 2009, in its annual report, the Census Bureau figured that the number of Americans without health insurance rose to 46.3 million last year as people started to lose jobs, while the poverty rate hit 13.2 percent – an 11-year high.

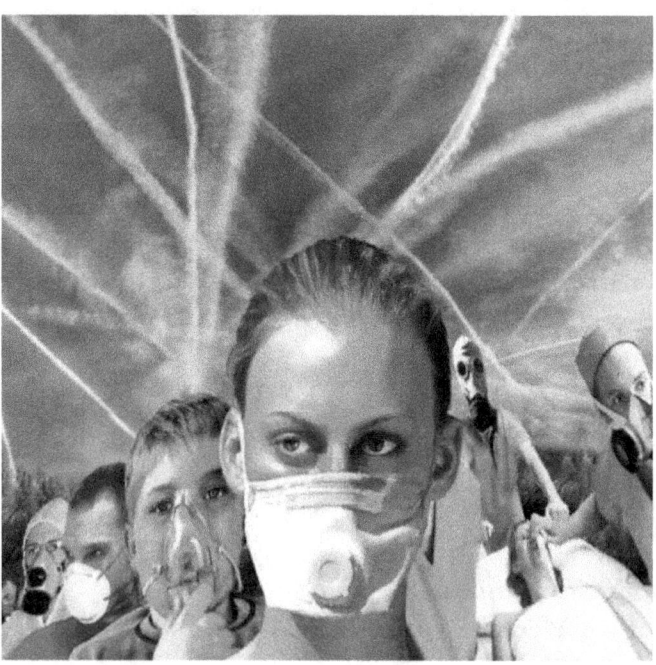

The report offers an overall idea of the economic well-being of American households for 2008. These figures come as the Congress engages in its debate over health care overhaul as President Barack Obama pleas to pass sweeping legislation. Ironically, these numbers have not captured the economic impact in the first half of 2009 as hundreds of thousands of Americans lost their jobs and along with it, their health insurance. Even President Obama acknowledged that the number of those without coverage may be considerably higher than the Census figures.

According to Obama: *The situation has grown worse over the last 12 months. It is estimated that the ranks of the uninsured have swelled by at least 6 million.*

These two figures speak sufficiently enough of the acuteness of the economic crisis that we are in. Jobs, health insurance and poverty rates are the few indices that speak of the wellbeing of people without any hidden nuances. It also means that life for the middle class had been hard. Very difficult indeed.

Incidentally, the US is the only developed nation that is yet to have a comprehensive national health plan for its citizens. Most Americans are forced to rely on private insurance – most often than not provided by their employers. However, not all employers provide insurance, especially for workers dwelling in the lower middle class, who anyways cannot afford a private insurance.

The figures depict that about 46.3 million people were uninsured in 2008. That is higher than the 45.7 million in 2007. The main reason for the increase is bound to be the steady erosion of health insurance provided by the employers. As consumer spending decreases, the companies face losses and ax its employees by removing health insurance cover. However, the silver lining is that the level remained below the peak of 47 million who were uninsured in 2006.

According to the figures:

- The percentage of Americans without health coverage rose to 15.4 percent, which is not much different from 15.3 percent in 2007.
- The nation's poverty rate increased to 13.2 percent – up from the 12.5 percent in 2007. This means that there were 39.8 million poor people, or, in other words, nearly one out of seven people in America lived in poverty in 2008. This is an increase of about 2.5 million from 2007 and attained the highest level since 1997. Based on a calculation that includes cash income before deductions for taxes, the official poverty

level is now $22,025 for a family of four. However, that level excludes capital gains accrued or accumulated wealth.

- The Census data also show that employment-based health insurance has declined from 177.4 million to 176.3 million. However, the number of people covered by government health insurance climbed from 83.0 million to 87.4 million.
- The number of uninsured children declined from 8.1 million in 2007 to 7.3 million in 2008. A decrease from 11.0 percent to 9.9 percent.
- The number of uninsured among the whites in America rose to 10.8 percent, or 21.3 million, an increase from 10.4 percent, or 20.5 million, in 2007.
- The condition of blacks, were not very different from 2007, at 19.1 percent and 7.3 million.
- The uninsured rate among the Asians in 2008 rose to 17.6 percent, up from 16.8 percent.
- The number of uninsured Hispanics was also not much different statistically in 2008, at 14.6 million. The percentage of uninsured Hispanics decreased to 30.7 percent in 2008, from 32.1 percent in 2007.

Although the decline in the uninsured is not to whooping extents, several analysts warned that this were likely to be just the tip of the iceberg; as unemployment rates are seen to be significantly higher in 2009. Based on current job losses, some researchers have made an estimate that the present-day number of uninsured is closer to 50 million.

Financial institutions are yet in terms to clean up their balance sheets. There have been layoffs in the housing industry, the airline industry, the car industry and other industries that are bound to contribute to future weakness. There seems to be uncertainty among the top think tank of the United States. After leading the Federal Reserve through a period of massive reductions in the and after intervening into areas of financial sector in ways that are reminiscent of the Great Depression, Chairman Bernanke has stated that maybe the Federal Reserve will have to look out after the decline in the value of the US dollar.

However, not just the Chairman, but several other members of the Federal Reserve have expressed doubts about how the Federal Reserve's actions. There have been concerns about the Federal Reserve lending to major securities firms and concerns about whether or not the Fed should actually be doing these things.

Apart from Barnanke, two other presidents of Federal Reserve have expressed similar concerns. President of the Federal Reserve Bank of Minneapolis, Gary Stern, questioned the expansion of the Fed's authority, while president of the Kansas City Federal Reserve bank. Thomas Hoenig, discussed about the threat of moral hazard in the financial system due to the Fed's actions.

In recent times, there has never been so much of public discussion about what the Federal Reserve is doing, has done or is supposed to do, by the individuals within the Federal Reserve System. These people have a responsibility for making the policy decisions that the Fed executes. So, a few eyebrows have been raised on the Fed's workings.

Maybe people are starting to see through the fraudulent institution that the Fed is. In recent times, the economy was booming and people were content enough to turn a deaf ear and a blind eye towards the actions of the Fed. But maybe the depression was the pinch the American people needed to wake them up from their daydreams and face harsh reality. The amassing of huge debt through the Fed had escaped the eyes of the public. But after the recession, Americans have begun to see the cause of the problem and the people responsible for the cause.

Looking at the condition of the financial system, one can see that foreclosures have remained high, and most probably will continue to rise. Bankruptcies have increased, and this also will probably continue. Charge offs towards credit card and debt are high and rising. In addition, if the economy is going to get softer with delinquencies and other financial dislocations increasing. The question remains as to how stable are the financial institutions of the United States?

Now, the state of the economy has started to show signs of growing weakness. The bad news is piling up, yet the economy seems to be hanging in there. On the other hand, unemployment figures are up and the impacts of the higher oil and gas prices seem to be spreading to more and major industries and hurting the middle and the lower middle class. Chairman Bernanke may express concern about the weakness in the value of the dollar, but not much can really be done to combat its falling value. The water has gone up the nose level, and the economy is bound to drown.

The United States cannot act to protect the value of the dollar simply because of the fragility of its economic and financial system while other major countries in the world now are indicating that they, in all likelihood, will raise interest rates in the future. If others do hike interest rates this can only put the United States in a more difficult position. This is because, if the Fed does need to act to further protect the economy or even if it does not move from the targets it now has set its eyes on, the weakness in the value of the dollar will only continue to increase. The actions of other nations (raising the rates of interest) will place the dollar in a relatively worse position than it is now.

This is a time when the world's only superpower has gone off on its own path. Now, when the United States is reaping the consequences of what it had sowed in the past, the only way others can contribute to helping it resolve its difficulties is to weaken their own discipline and act in a way not consistent with the long-term welfare of the people of US. It is a situation where, although being a superpower and having the capacity to pinpoint and destroy a bunker tens and thousands of miles away, it cannot take care of its own people. It can do nothing when, due to its own flawed policy, people suffer, become poor or are squeezed to inhuman extents.

FINANCIAL DISASTER: THE ROAD AHEAD

A situation of cash crunch looms perilously over Uncle Sam. Does this ring a bell? It sounds almost hackneyed or even cliché when one talks about when his friend or relative fell short of cash accumulating debts! Fat pay packets, job with a multi national company seem lucrative enough for people to go for an expensive luxury car, Mercedes or BMW, a vacation home and a palatial bungalow. Things look to be going fine till one fine day the job is lost while savings get depleted in a few months. The vacation home cannot be sold off as the real estate values have dropped below the mortgage value. A millionaire a year ago, bankrupt the next.

Such situations arise as the ordinary US citizen is not concerned enough about the credit bubble bursting, which would ultimately lead to deflation. While savings across America are at dismal levels, debt per individual is at its peak. Credit bubble has been a recent phenomenon from the year 2000 due to an oversupply of credit. During the year of the Y2K bug, the Federal Reserve is known to have flooded the market with credit. Consider this factoid; President George Bush borrowed almost $ 1 trillion during the course of his first five years in the Oval Office. This debt was far more that money borrowed by all the previous 43 Presidents put together! In a way, Bush helped the economy as the resultant credit bubble helped keep the volatile stock market in check and prevent it from collapsing irrevocably. The credit bubble had also led to a boom in the real estate. That was the good news. The really bad news is that this debt must be re-paid one way or the other.

This is akin to what happened after 9/11. Back then the Federal Reserve Bank Chairman, Mr. Greenspan flooded the markets with easy credit. While disproportionate credit and cut in interest rates do keep the economy afloat, they also beget debt trap. Serious problems arise when debt cannot be paid back or credit get cut off leading to a rather precarious situation. And this is what caused the problem. A short squeeze too can set in that is if the credit bubble bursts, it could spark off a short squeeze (a trader jargon). Short squeeze is a condition when the price of a stock is high prompting several traders to short the stock ("short the stock" means that borrowing shares from an investment house, selling them and eagerly watching if the share prices will drop). When stock prices drop traders buy back the shares and hand them back to the investment. But what happens when it happens the other way round, it becomes a short squeeze. This is what will happen to America when the credit bubble will burst.

When can a short squeeze occur? Will it affect the dollar? I believe so. These are scary questions, questions which are on the mind of the entire middle class. If a short squeeze happens to the US dollar that would mean that the lenders would have forced the debtors to pay in cash. A possible scenario worth considering, one can safely say. In such circumstances, assets would need to be sold off at ridiculously low rates to generate the cash needs. With the credit markets going for a toss, there is a strong likelihood that there could millions of American middle class families who thought they were rich but turned out to be poor. This could propel the lending rates vertically straight out of the roof in the process making dollar more valuable and resulting in a deflation. We all know that the credit bubble has already burst and deflation is not looking good either. The point of fact is that inflation is easier to control or curtail than deflation. The moral of the story, in the current scenario, cash is a life saver.

That the credit bubble has burst indicates that credit has disappeared but people have stopped spending and started hoarding cash. As money is the stimulus for any economy, when credit is wiped and money (cash) is idling parked somewhere, the economy slows and recession or even a depression ensues. The good thing about all this is that prices of everything and anything will only come down and good deals can be struck provided there is cash in hand. Also given the lack of direction as far as markets are concerned and high interest debts, it makes senses to set aside some cash for investments. The short squeeze on cash is, many analysts believe, a temporary phase that will soon be over. And the dollar may not continue its fall after all. The middle classes need to study the market and trends carefully before making their investments. But in the same breath, when people purchase consumer items such as a new car or use debt to finance some shopping or spending spree and when these items lose their value due to drop in the dollar value, consumer lose both ways.

Generally, the trend is that Americans continue to buy more consumer durables even while the value of the goods they recently bought has nose dived due to a weak dollar. The smart investors knew the right thing to do. These smart investors are those who invested in stocks of oil and gas, gold, real estate and silver ahead of time. A grave anxiety rests among the citizens of the world who may any time soon get tired of sickening fiscal mismanagement by the US. In order to repose faith in the American currency, interest rates need to soar. What will then happen is that paper assets such as US bonds, mutual funds, stocks and savings will drop in value whereas real estate prices will increase. This is will lead to a state of affairs where there will still be paper assets and real estate prices will also rise.

Another point of view is that Americans do not invest in gold and silver as they have still failed to realize the value of these precious metals.

Currencies may fail, they may collapse but gold and silver will also act a bargaining chip as they are the real money. Dollar is only a currency after all. The government of any country today has no option but to print currency but they all must realize that it only leads to inflation which would further shoot up the value of gold and silver.

What is the New Administration doing?

As this economic turmoil continues to boil, let us take a look what the President thinks about it. He had come out in the open and had ridiculed his opponents and had won an election mainly on the basis on the economic blunders his opponents made. It might be interesting to look back on what he had said before he became the president. Underneath is an excerpt from *The Independent* which was published on September 16th 2008:

Tuesday, 16 September 2008: Barack Obama has expanded his call for stricter control of the US financial sector into an across-the-board attack on the laissez-faire economics championed by Ronald Reagan, pursued by President George Bush for the past eight years, and embraced by the Republican candidate for the White House, John McCain. The Democratic presidential candidate said he was not blaming Mr McCain in person for "the most serious financial crisis since the Great Depression" , but "the economic philosophy he subscribes to," based on tax cuts for the wealthy and the habit of "ignoring economic problems until they spiralled into crises".

During the Bush years, that philosophy insisted that "even commonsense regulations are unneccessary and unwise", with the result that the administration had sat on its hands as problems turned into crises – the latest being the convulsions on Wall Street. Whatever its ultimate consequences, the crisis now shaking Wall Street seems bound to lead to greater federal government regulation of the financial sector

… Indeed, events have forced even the anti-regulatory and anti-interventionist Bush administration to change tack, with a $150bn (£84bn) stimulus package earlier this year to boost the economy, and assistance for some of the millions of Americans facing the loss of their homes to foreclosure. The scope of the measures has been criticised, but the change of direction is indisputable …

… The Lehman bankruptcy, Mr. McCain said, was but "the latest reminder of ineffective regulation and management" that plagued the financial sector. A McCain-Palin White House would replace the "outdated and ineffective patchwork quilt of regulatory oversight in Washington" and bring "transparency and accountability to Wall Street"…

… That certainly is what Americans want.

"America will never be destroyed from the outside. If we falter and lose our freedoms, it will be because we destroyed ourselves." – **Abraham Lincoln**

WHAT SHOULD YOU BE DOING?

There is a saying in Chinese: "Give a man a fish and feed him a day. Teach the man fishing and feed him a life." Guess what, we're trying to teach people how to fish for a better tomorrow. Cliché, yeah but given the current circumstances, reality bites. Typically, the motto of the US economy, hitherto, has been: live today to see tomorrow. It is time American people wake up and realize that whatever they have borrowed had been at the expense of their future generations. The future generations will have to pay up for what they have done; or to be more precise, for what America has consumed. And only a sound and realistic knowledge of the economic situation will save the Americans, and especially the middle class from going down the drain. So plan today, for a better tomorrow.

Do not invest in fiat currency for it will fall like a house of cards. Invest in gold or precious metals. They are precious as you cannot physically produce them on the go in order to meet your needs. The dollar is not as precious it once used to be. The dollar is in a free fall and most of the central banks of various countries are shifting from dollar to a more stable currency, including stocking up on gold. On the domestic front, the policymakers are producing the dollar and by controlling the money supply, they control the economy. Therefore, don't dance to their tunes, especially if you're not counting on pushing daisies from six feet under anytime soon.

America, as a country and a nation is poised at the verge of a historical moment. As more and more people wake up from the decades of slumber that they have been in, their action is going to shape the future of the country. The truth has been hidden for too long a time and it is now an open secret that American policymakers had been cheating the people by giving them false hopes that everything is hunky dory. It is not. Do not depend on the politicians to tell you what is good for you, instead, identify them yourself. Zone out the political double speak and decipher the truth behind the lies, before it's too late to do anything. It's time for Americans to stop politicians from playing them like dummies at the end of a string. It's time they realized that it's in the hands of the common mass to get the country out of debt.

Today, America is no longer free. They are financially dependent and indebted. The Federal Reserve, the Builderberg Group and the entire Elites have sold off the very independence that Washington and Lincoln had fought for. Therefore, it is about what America had stood for all these years. Our threat is not hiding in some cave in Afghanistan or Pakistan as many of the mass media would like you to believe so that the you will quit asking about medical or social security. It is more economic than anything else. Face the stark truth people, it's staring right back at you. America will not be free ever again until it is free from all of its debts and until the mass awakes to the truth.

LET the Truth be Exposed!
Visit <u>MyInfo4U.net</u> where the truth is exposed...

A Special Thanks and courtesy to David Dees from Deesillustration. com for providing the illustrations for this book.